Personalized D
Advertisin

Personalized Digital Advertising

How Data and Technology Are Transforming How We Market

Diaz Nesamoney

Publisher: Paul Boger
Editor-in-Chief: Amy Neidlinger
Acquisitions Editor: Charlotte Maiorana
Operations Specialist: Jodi Kemper
Cover Designer: Alan Clements
Managing Editor: Kristy Hart
Senior Project Editor: Betsy Gratner
Copy Editor: Kitty Wilson
Proofreader: Chuck Hutchinson
Indexer: Tim Wright
Compositor: Nonie Ratcliff
Manufacturing Buyer: Dan Uhrig

© 2015 by Diaz Nesamoney
Published by Pearson Education, Inc.
Old Tappan, New Jersey 07675

For information about buying this title in bulk quantities, or for special sales opportunities (which may include electronic versions; custom cover designs; and content particular to your business, training goals, marketing focus, or branding interests), please contact our corporate sales department at corpsales@pearsoned.com or (800) 382-3419.

For government sales inquiries, please contact governmentsales@pearsoned.com.

For questions about sales outside the U.S., please contact international@pearsoned.com.

Company and product names mentioned herein are the trademarks or registered trademarks of their respective owners.

Printed in the United States of America

First Printing April 2015

ISBN-10: 0-13-403010-9
ISBN-13: 978-0-13-403010-4

Pearson Education LTD.
Pearson Education Australia PTY, Limited
Pearson Education Singapore, Pte. Ltd.
Pearson Education Asia, Ltd.
Pearson Education Canada, Ltd.
Pearson Educación de Mexico, S.A. de C.V.
Pearson Education—Japan
Pearson Education Malaysia, Pte. Ltd.

Library of Congress Control Number: 2015931957

This book is dedicated to the "mad" men and women who continue to work diligently to make advertising beautiful, fun, relevant, and engaging. Whether on TV, print, digital, or new media we haven't even thought about, advertising needs to remain all of the above to contribute to a brand's success.

Contents

Foreword

I first met Diaz at an industry meeting at the Interactive Advertising Bureau held by Peter Minnium (who writes in Chapter 23, "Industry Perspectives"). This meeting was a combination of creatives and technologists whose mission was to address the challenges that were ahead of us related to the proliferation of screens. The problem at that time was addressing mobile and native content, but we'd soon determine that was just the tip of the iceberg. What new approaches would we take as an industry? How would those affect creative development, media placement, and measurement?

In the early meetings, Diaz and I were instant teammates in a battle for which we had not enlisted. It was called the "technologists" against the "creatives." The notion of "dynamic creative" was a slap in the face to any decent creative person's skillset. The heated arguments that ensued were about the future of creativity and continued constrained resources against our known digital future of screens.

The arguments have not gone away, and they shouldn't, as it is an important debate to be had. However, the debate of "or" itself seems fleeting. The debate should not be creative *or* technology. Instead, we should seek the right equilibrium of creative *and* technology.

Technology is changing the way consumers interact with content and media. Messaging on the next billion devices will look quite different than our approach to the current landscape of screens. Specific and structured standard ad sizes grew our world up until now; for example 30s, 60s, and even 90s in TV or 300×250s or 468×90s in display. However, as we all know, "what got us here won't get us there."

Nonstandard media formats will continue to rise, requiring us to rethink standards with the notion of specifications, variables (creative, content, context, and consumer), predictive algorithms, and machine learning.

Key technology and consumer growth areas in our world, like smartphone meeting telematics, the gamification of everything, location fueling the Internet of Things (and Everything), and the rise of the cognitive interface, will push us to evolve our approaches to creating messages. In all cases, we will have more devices, more form-factors with which to connect to consumers, and a continued lack of standards.

We must understand how to paint brand messages in new ways. This will prove to be challenging in our existing systems as the "tools and processes were built with the assumption of a static ad that remains the same through a campaign" (as Diaz noted). Development of a dynamic creative is challenging because the dimension of variability must be considered. However, if we look at other models to understand how to handle variability, we might be able to stretch our creative palette to its potential.

What if we applied the thinking behind a popular coding site called ifttt.com (If This Then That), where the tagline reads: "Put the Internet to work for you"? This messaging is profound. What if we let the Internet works for us, rather than be a resource drain to us?

Here's how it works: The site helps create useful combinations of coding functions into one statement called a "recipe." The recipe has two functions: a trigger and an action. The trigger helps us understand what something did. The action helps us program what we should do about it. Pretty simple, actually. By applying the notion of recipes to the concept of dynamic creative, we have a message fabric and a mechanism to reach people not just on new screens but also in new functionalities within those screens.

We are experiencing a point in time where many things are colliding to create an environment for not just a new standard but a holistic shift in our thinking. This is happening *now*. The explosion of new screens, content layers, and messaging moments like in-image, augmented reality, and the Internet of Things are potential moments to expand the brand fabric and require unique assets for messaging to consumers.

This is our present and our future. If we become masters at leveraging personalized, dynamic, and native messaging approaches and learnings, we will best prepare ourselves for these new places to advertise.

Cary Tilds
Chief Innovation Officer
GroupM
@ctilds
www.linkedin.com/in/carytilds/

Acknowledgments

I would like to acknowledge the many people who inspired me and supported me throughout this project. In the midst of my busy schedule as CEO of a rapidly growing company; maddening travel each week between the San Francisco Bay Area, New York, Los Angeles, and India; trying to be a good dad to two young kids; and keeping my commitments and passion as director of a charitable foundation, it was quite a miracle that this book actually came together when it did. I now know it takes a team and starts at home.

First, I thank my wife, Usha, without whom I would not have been bold enough to even undertake this project. It came about at a time when neither of us could imagine finding even an hour a week to do anything new. In spite of her very busy and seemingly endless responsibilities, she always seems to be able to support me in what I do.

I was also inspired by my kids to write this book. Our daughter Sophia published her first book, *The Other Side of Carroll* (now available through Amazon), when she was 9. Our son Sean, who is now 9 and not to be outdone, is finishing up his first book. I also want to acknowledge both of them for being patient with me each time they were told "Daddy is finishing his book" when they wanted me to help with homework or go out and play with them.

Thanks to my colleagues at work—Naren Nachiappan, Sanjay Dahiya, Jaimie Villacarlos, and Daniel Green, the "dream team" who helped productize a lot of what you will read in this book, were an amazing source of ideas and insights into how personalized advertising should be done.

Thanks to my admin and my company's people manager, social manager, and trusted confidante of over 11 years, Claudia. She was always there 7×24 to make sure I was able to make progress with the book in spite of my grueling travel schedules. I can't think of anyone else I could call late evening on my way to the airport, saying I needed a power supply to finish my book on my long flight to India. She pulled it off, finding a store that was open and couriering it to me just before I had to board my flight.

Thanks to my mentors in the subject matter of personalized advertising. Each of them has a tremendous wealth of industry knowledge and freely brainstormed with me and generously gave of their time to not only share their perspectives but also contribute a few paragraphs to the book. Thanks to Cary Tilds, chief innovation officer, GroupM; Gregg Colvin, chief operating officer, Universal McCann; Peter Minnium, head of brand initiatives, IAB; Gowthaman Ragothaman, chief operating officer, Mindshare APAC; and Karin Timpone, global marketing officer, Marriott International. They all gave me amazing anecdotes and insights into why embracing personalized advertising is important for marketers.

I also want to acknowledge the amazing team at Jivox, who have turned what were just ideas a few years ago into products, customers, and campaigns. We have broken new ground every day as we have implemented a lot of what I talk about in this book. I also want to thank them for listening to me patiently as I rambled on and on about how important and big personalized advertising was going to be.

Last but not least, I want to thank my editor, Charlotte Maiorana, who found me and believed I was the right person to write this book and gave me some great insights on writing my very first book. She was also patient with me when I had to extend a few deadlines to make it to the finish line.

About the Author

Diaz Nesamoney is an accomplished technology entrepreneur who founded three successful technology companies. Currently Diaz is Founder, President, and CEO of Jivox, a company that provides a technology platform for personalized advertising. He was previously Cofounder, President, and Chief Operating Officer at Informatica (NASDAQ:INFA), which he took from a startup to a publicly traded company in 1999. Informatica pioneered data integration software as a category and is now the market leader with more than $1 billion in revenue and a $4.5 billion market capitalization. Before founding Jivox, he founded Celequest, raised more than $20 million in venture capital, and served as its CEO until early 2007, when the company was acquired by Cognos/IBM. Celequest introduced the market's first business intelligence and analytics appliance, a disruptive innovation that led to its acquisition. Diaz is a board member of the American India Foundation, a leading international development organization charged with the mission of accelerating social and economic change in India. Diaz is also a member of the Board of Trustees at the World Affairs Council. Diaz holds a Masters degree in Computer Science from the Birla Institute of Technology and Science in India and is the holder of six technology patents.

1

The Talking Billboard

In the 2002 movie *Minority Report*, Tom Cruise walks into a mall and is greeted by "live" billboards that address him by name and show him outfits he will likely be interested in. The billboards do it by scanning his retina. (Turns out it's someone else's retina, but you'll have to watch the movie to know why.)

In many ways, as advertising has gone from traditional media to new media, it has not changed very much. When I was growing up, my first exposure to advertising was posters on walls everywhere I went and a few large billboards advertising everything from toothpaste to cars. The idea of marketing via posters was simple: Buy enough of them at the lowest possible price per poster and get them out in as many places as possible. It was about two things: volume and price. Advertisers sought the highest possible volume at the lowest possible price. Brand managers were taught in business school that it was all about coming up with a clever tagline or jingle and trying to get as many people to see and hear it as possible.

Along came newspapers, magazines, and TV—first one channel in black and white and then three channels and then cable with hundreds of channels. The same sort of growth happened with radio.

Marketers repeated the same formula used in advertising. To be sure, creative agencies came up with more clever ways to get the message across and also utilized new media like video for TV commercials and audio for radio, but the idea remained the same: Get your message out to as many people as possible for the lowest possible cost.

Despite dramatic advances in digital media, devices, and new types of media like social media, most digital ads today don't look very different or behave any differently than the billboards that have been around since the beginning of advertising. Display banner ads are simply sized-down versions of those billboards. And they're only about as effective as billboards, judging by the click-through and engagement rates that display banners are delivering to brands.

Digital media presents immense opportunities to not only make significantly more functional billboards but also smarter billboards that understand consumers' interests and tailor advertising and messaging directly to their needs. This is a largely untapped opportunity for marketers.

For some time, pundits have predicted that advertising will become much more personalized and relevant. While we don't quite have billboards scanning our retinas, it seems clear that a big wave of personalization driven by the vast amounts of data we now have is about to sweep through all of marketing.

Several factors have come together in recent years to create this inflection point—some technological, some consumer behavioral changes, and some to do with the widespread use of social media. These advances have made it possible to embark on personalizing marketing inexpensively and at scale.

Mobile Devices Become Personal Media and Sharing Devices

The biggest change in consumer behavior has been a greater willingness to share personal information. Social media has accelerated this trend, and people now share online anything and everything, including who their friends are, their likes and dislikes, where they live, where they've visited, what they've said, and what they've watched. This is a big cultural and perhaps generational shift in thinking to a general openness to sharing personal information in return for a more personalized experience.

Many years ago, people worried about others tracking them and knowing exactly where they were. Today we freely let apps like Uber, OpenTable, Yelp, and others use our location to help us quickly get a car service, make reservations, or find a restaurant nearby. We even deliberately "check in" in many mobile apps, telling everyone where we are. Many years ago, we worried about video rental information getting into the wrong hands. Today our Facebook and YouTube pages are filled with video content we watch and let the world know we watch. In some cases—as with Uber, OpenTable, and Yelp using location information—users get something in return for their sharing; but even in cases where they don't seem to get anything, users seem more than willing to share information about themselves.

The rapid proliferation of mobile devices has essentially served to personalize our digital media consumption. Instead of a family sitting around a TV, we now have our own personal palm-sized TVs available all the time. Rather than huddle around a radio, we each have a Pandora account to listen to our own tunes (nobody needs to know you secretly listen to ABBA). Now that we can watch whatever we like on Netflix, there's no more fighting over the TV remote.

Such technological change has spurred the movement toward more personalized experiences for users. In addition to mobile devices becoming personal media devices, they have also quickly become "sharing devices." Through the use of social media, these devices have unleashed a torrent of location, preference, and other kinds of data volunteered by users. This data has become a treasure trove that marketers can use to personalize experiences.

Recently, the explosion of connected devices variously called "wearables" or "the Internet of things" is creating vast amounts of personal data that adds to the arsenal of data that marketers now have to work with.

Computing power and bandwidth have also increased to a point where tasks that used to take several minutes to hours—like executing an algorithm to match a user to his or her user profile—can now be done in milliseconds. Cloud computing capabilities have also significantly reduced the costs of storing, retrieving, and processing the massive amounts of data needed to effectively personalize advertising.

Marketing Starts to Take Data Seriously

Data has always been viewed as an afterthought in marketing. Marketers were used to doing post-analysis of campaign results, research, and sales data to try to understand how to market to their prospects and customers. Data traditionally wasn't used much for delivering campaigns and targeting and personalizing experiences for customers. But big changes are happening as we speak. Marketers now view data as a strategic asset that should be utilized aggressively as a key part of their arsenal.

In the past year, according to Forrester Research, marketers' interest in and spending for data and analytics has increased from 8% to 12%. Hardly an article today doesn't mention the role of "Big Data" in marketing. The good news is also that Big Data and analytics are being viewed as core marketing infrastructure, much like an accounting system is for the finance function within a company.

The investments in data and analytics are likely to get marketing teams the kinds of information they can use and rely on to deliver personalized services to their customers. The investments will need to be significant, but they can and will be viewed as capital investments that will enable these companies to better engage with their customers in a more intelligent fashion.

In the past year, Oracle Corporation—the largest enterprise database and applications company—acquired BlueKai and Datalogix, two Big Data companies focused on providing data for targeting and personalizing advertisements. This reflects the growing appetite marketing organizations and CMOs have to spend on marketing technology and infrastructure.

There's an API for That

Remember the Apple ad that said "there's an app for that"? We can now say "there's an API for that." APIs (or application programming interfaces) have been significantly important to the rapid evolution and adoption of technology in the media and advertising industry. The successes of Facebook, Apple, and Google as media/technology companies can definitely be attributed to their heavy and aggressive investments in APIs that have allowed third-party apps and platforms to plug into and help grow their ecosystems. In the digital advertising arena, too, APIs have played a key role.

An API called openRTB has been largely responsible for the ability for brands to buy and sell media programmatically. This API allows sellers and buyers of media to communicate electronically about availability of inventory, ask and bid prices, information about the inventory itself, etc. All this has been done using a set of standard APIs, and it has enabled programmatic media buying and selling to scale and gain adoption rapidly despite the varied media suppliers, supply-side and demand-side platforms, and exchanges that are invariably involved in such media transactions.

In the world of personalized advertising, APIs can now tell us everything from where a user is located to what the local weather is like to what movie theater is playing a particular movie. All these APIs serve up data that can be used for more effective personalization.

APIs also allow for interoperability and ease of integration between the pieces of software that have to come together to make personalization work. For example, most data management platforms have APIs by which dynamic/personalized ad platforms can fetch data to personalize ads.

Social Media Teaches Us Marketing

Brands have been inspired by the way Facebook and Twitter have been able to offer them ad products with very fine-grained targeting and real-time messaging capabilities. Today, within a few minutes, a brand can think up a message or creative idea it wants to communicate to a very specific audience and have it sent to that audience within minutes. The question many brands are rightfully asking is "Why can't I do this across all my media?" For various reasons, including especially the limited types of ad formats offered by social media platforms, brands want to use those same techniques of micro-messaging and real-time marketing across their display advertising.

Marketers are also realizing that the traditional path to purchase has changed significantly due to the impact of social media and mobile devices. Now consumers can make purchase decisions in real time without following the traditional paths to purchase. This means brands also have to be able to be in that purchase path in real time with something to say or offer that will tilt the purchase decision in their direction.

A lot of the key ingredients are in place to make personalized advertising a reality, so what's missing? As in any other emerging area in digital advertising, there's a lot of confusing terminology and technologies, as well as a lack of APIs and standards for how data, content, and ad serving platforms come together to make it all happen. This is all changing as we speak, and it is already evident that marketers are taking this opportunity head on and collaborating with technologists to make their desires reality.

This book examines the rationale, opportunity, process, and technology involved in personalizing advertising. I am hopeful that it will be a handy reference to marketers and technologists for personalizing interactions with customers. As you will see in the examples in the book and anecdotes from some industry leaders, personalized advertising is already well on its way to reinventing how we market.

2

Reach vs. Relevance

Marketers have traditionally played with two levers to influence buyers: They have tried to get as much reach as possible (i.e., exposing customers to the brand), and they have tried to get customers engaged by being as relevant as possible to their needs (or at least portraying the product as being relevant).

Achieving reach, of course, was all about using media that had a lot of reach—traditionally TV, newspapers, radio, and so on and more recently ad networks, exchanges, and programmatic buying platforms. Marketers tried to use low-cost media to achieve greater reach for a given budget.

Relevance in traditional media was largely achieved by matching it with content. For example, marketers could assume by association that folks who watched the *Cosby Show* were probably a household with kids, while folks who watched MTV were probably single or married with no kids. Likewise, marketers concluded that folks who watched the Discovery Channel were more likely to travel, and people who watched CNBC were either in the financial services business or had a level of wealth to invest.

The problem was that highly relevant shows often came at the cost of reach. Specialized audiences came at a high cost: Either reach was compromised by using media with small specialized audiences or, if a cable network had both significant reach and a target audience of interest, the cost of media was significant.

There was a reason the term *mass media* was frequently used to the describe TV and print advertising—and even posters and billboards. They were all media designed for mass communication of the same message, which was generally one size fits all. Today, while there are several flavors of the *Wall Street Journal* and CNN in different regions, print and TV have struggled to deliver any kind of customized media experience to consumers.

Without customized media, of course, there was no customized audience and, therefore, no advertising that could be customized to even a small audience—let alone to an individual.

Creating audience engagement when advertising could not achieve more precise targeting and messaging was largely done by creative means. Creative agencies had to come up with clever lines, visually appealing creative assets, and so on to try to engage users.

When digital advertising began, creativity continued to play the role it has had in traditional media. Unlike with traditional media (especially TV), though, digital ads were often placed on the "rails" of a page, in standard-sized boxes (the so-called IAB standard ad formats), and this often caused users to simply ignore the ads. The ad formats themselves were very small—300×250 pixels, 300×600 pixels, 728×90 pixels, and 160×600 pixels—hardly a canvas within which much creativity was possible. These ads led to significant drops in user engagement. When publisher websites were quickly filled with small and annoying banner ads, users' brains simply tuned out these ads, which were neither interesting nor relevant. Furthermore, many of the ads were delivered in such a manner that users often didn't even see the ads, much less engage with them.

The only way for publishers and brands to get around this was to try to invent clever and more intrusive ways to get attention. Many publishers offered up "custom ad formats," which included formats like page skins, "interstitials" that blocked users from the content they were about to read or watch, and large "takeovers" that appeared out of nowhere and forced a message on the user. The IAB (Interactive Advertising Bureau), in response to the demand for such attention-grabbing ad formats, came up with the IAB "Rising Star" ad formats. These "high-impact" ad formats were much larger in size and allowed for a much more expansive, creative canvas to try to engage users.

Just as Rising Star formats were gaining a lot of traction, with many brands choosing these richer, bigger, and more impactful ad formats, a big change occurred in digital media: programmatic media buying. This change created massive media-buying efficiencies. This, however, had a very significant side effect in that these platforms did not support the high-impact formats. The reasons had to do with the often-challenging process of delivering these indirectly via the "programmatic platform plumbing" and also the inevitable lack of scale in buying brought about by the scarcity of inventory that could support these kinds of formats on a specific publisher's site.

The scarcity of inventory for high-impact ad formats had to do with the fact that these formats were large, and often a web page could support at most one or two such large ad formats, while it could support several of the "IAB standard" ad formats.

Brands started a very significant shift of media spend to programmatic platforms, and their ad formats are now shifting back to the standard smaller-size banner ads. This has the effect of again making it difficult to create engagement using creativity as a lever.

So the battle to create engagement from users clearly cannot be fought with creativity alone because the creativity canvas once again is being reduced to small boxes and rectangles on the sides of a publisher's page. The other way to create engagement is, of course, by making sure an ad is relevant to the user and that it markets to the user in a very personalized way. Targeted media buys get us partway there, but personalization at scale is what puts brands as close to the one-on-one relationship they have sought with users.

Traditional media simply could not deliver any form of personalization. This was primarily due to three reasons:

- Traditional media is not interactive and therefore has no way of registering user preferences, interests, etc., to personalize media or advertising.
- There was no way to transmit or publish customized content to each user in a scalable and cost-effective manner.
- While some forms of data existed in cable set-top boxes and the cable distribution systems, the proprietary systems and heavy regulations around the cable industry have generally prevented the data from being used.

With digital media, none of these limitations exist. With digital media, we are able to record and easily access user preference data. What's more, the amount of finer-grained data related to preferences and interests has grown rapidly. In addition, new kinds of data—like data about a user's environment, thanks largely to the use of mobile devices and social media—are adding a wealth of data that can be used to make digital advertising smarter and much more relevant to each user.

The second limitation—the inability to personalize and publish media content and advertising to a user—is now no longer such a limitation. Personalization data is becoming available through a variety of data management platforms as well as first-party data that brands already have access to: New dynamic ad serving platforms and software for developing personalized content and ads are making it easy to publish such personalized content and advertisements to users at scale. Fueled by APIs and standards for how these technologies and platforms work together, personalized advertising is now quickly becoming a reality.

In the next few years, brands are going to be tasked with creating more relevant advertising and getting away from just blasting largely irrelevant ads and generic copy to millions of people. Brands that take the time and effort to create relevance using personalization and relevant content will win out by creating both media efficiency (i.e., the right message to the right person at the right time) and also engagement, as users see ads as being informative and giving them something of value.

Programmatic media buying is not only here to stay but may be the way most media is bought and sold. This creates an imperative and urgency for brands to get more intelligent and creative not just in the sense of pretty images and visuals but also in messaging and relevance.

There is a big shift occurring—from viewing advertising in a "broadcast" mindset that came from traditional media to a new "publishing" mindset, where the onus is on the brand to keep the audience engaged with useful and relevant content. We can no longer count on limited choice or lack of choice as a way to keep users engaged.

3

Digital Disruption: The Proliferation and Personalization of Media

The Internet, whether invented by Al Gore or not, spurred the possibility of customizing content and media to users. When the Internet started to become popular, instead of having 300 channels of TV and often saying "there is nothing good on TV," consumers could dial in and download or access content they wanted. The tremendous initial successes of dial-up content services like AOL and CompuServe proved that consumers really wanted to be able to select the content they wanted to view, and they wanted to do it on their schedule, not on the schedule of a TV program guide.

Portals like Yahoo, MSN, and AOL produced vast amounts of news, sports, and other entertainment content and allowed users to choose the content they wanted to consume and when to consume it. Everything had changed.

It didn't just stop there. Very quickly literally thousands and then millions of websites began to offer broad and sometimes very narrow content (a site for Siamese cat lovers, anyone?). The era of mass media was ending, and a big transition to "customized" media was under way. This movement, which started in the late 1990s and had its first big bubble and "peak" during the dot-com bubble of 2000, was in fact the first of several upheavals the media and advertising industry would undergo, thanks to the introduction of digitally produced and distributed content and media.

The first website went live in 1991; in 1992 there were 10 websites; and in 1993 there were 130. In 1999 there were 3 million websites, and by 2000, that number had jumped to 17 million. The billionth website in the world went live in September 2014. In some ways there was not only a shift going on in media consumption from traditional media to digital media but there was actually an increase in media consumption due to the ready availability of media in places other than the family room.

Prior to the Internet, media consumption while people were at work was minimal because TV watching and newspaper and magazine reading were not easy to do at work. When the Internet came to workplaces, people could surf the web whenever they took a break from work; they could do everything from reading news to watching sports to being entertained—all from the convenience of their desk.

The next big change was the introduction of laptops, which suddenly made the Internet portable. No longer did you have to be sitting in front of your TV at home or your desk at work; your media could travel with you on your laptop, as long as you had a Wi-Fi connection.

An important change that happened here is that media consumption became personalized. There was no more fighting over the remote; everyone could have his or her own choices. Interestingly, while many predicted the death of TV, these new ways of delivering media didn't entirely take away from TV but simply allowed us all to consume media even when we were not in front of our TVs.

For marketers, at first the Internet seemed like a great new medium to use for marketing. However, the very first problem with media delivered via the Internet is the significant fragmentation of audiences across websites. There were now not 300 channels but 300 million—and very quickly over 1 billion. This posed an immediate problem for marketers trying to leverage the medium: How do you ensure that you are delivering advertising to a relevant audience when your audience is so significantly fragmented? You couldn't buy media for a specific "cable channel" or a "sports section" at scale.

A number of media aggregators eventually cropped up. Ad exchanges and ad networks essentially helped solve the reach problem first by aggregating media across several thousand smaller sites and making it easier for brands to achieve their reach goals with a single media buy. This still left open the issue of how to achieve greater relevance and to ensure that the right audience was being reached.

To address the relevance issue, aggregators started organizing websites into "audience segments," which made it easier for brands to buy, say "auto enthusiasts." This was the first time marketers were able to see how technology combined with digital media could give them a great way to achieve both reach and relevance goals in a world of increasingly fragmented media.

While laptops and Wi-Fi significantly personalized media, there was yet another big change underway, and Steve Jobs saw it coming. While everyone saw wireless networks as being designed for making phone calls first and then maybe media, Steve Jobs put media first—ahead of even making phone calls. As someone once joked, the iPhone was a great phone if you didn't have to make phone calls; as Steve Jobs would say, it was an "insanely great" media device. Thousands bought the cool-looking phone and discovered a phenomenal portable and highly personal media device.

In 2014, the rapid growth of mobile devices reached a very important milestone: For the first time ever, more tablet devices were shipped than PCs. If we thought media was fragmented before— across millions of websites— this made it so dispersed that it was becoming impossible to comprehend the implications.

Just when we thought we were done with disruption of media, another big shift in digital media came with the rapid and dizzying growth in the use of social media by consumers. Social media created yet another form of digital media and still more fragmentation of media. What became even more bewildering for marketers was the crossover between social media and mobile—and a whole new world of mobile apps, which was clearly distinct from websites and web browsing experiences.

Social media also brought about a dramatic change in consumer behavior in that it appeared to have unlocked an innate desire in people to want to share things. YouTube, interestingly, was the first of this kind of "social media," though at that time various names like "user-generated content" were being used to describe the phenomenon. But no matter the terminology, YouTube really gave the media and advertising industry the first inkling that, privacy concerns aside, people really wanted to tell everyone—not just their friends—about themselves. Mobile devices fueled this fire by making it easy to take pictures, check in, update statuses, post, tweet, pin, etc., easily and conveniently via mobile devices.

All this posting and sharing had another effect in growing media availability and consumption. Facebook created a new category of media that had not even been thought about as media. People uploaded pictures, shared content, uploaded videos, etc. About 300 million images are uploaded to Facebook each day, and 4.75 *billion* pieces of content are shared by Facebook users each day.

Social media has successfully created even more media. This new kind of media is also much more personal. Each user has a "timeline" consisting of media shared and media that has been liked. In the process of sharing and liking content and media, consumers tell media companies—and often the rest of the world—everything there is to know about them. Suddenly, after marketers had spent years trying to figure out how to build profiles of users and their online habits, users had decided to just volunteer all this data and information.

While many marketers saw these new forms and channels of media consumption as simply marketing channels and started using terms like *multi-channel marketing* to describe the need to reach audiences across such media channels, many missed a perhaps bigger opportunity for increasing relevance of advertising that these big changes in digital media were presenting.

Each consumption point of digital media was also creating preference data where users were essentially not only sharing or selecting media, they were effectively also sharing information about themselves—their likes, dislikes, and other information that could be used to create more personalized media experiences for them.

When you log into Netflix or Amazon, you immediately notice that both services have essentially analyzed items you have viewed or purchased in the past and created recommendations based on your history. This idea of personalizing media or product choices was pioneered in the early days of e-commerce and is very prevalent today—but only in the world of media and e-commerce sites.

While media companies started trying to personalize media for their users, a bigger problem had emerged for marketers: It was no longer possible to rely simply on "targeting"—that is, purchasing media that was contextually relevant to the audience.

The way media companies and e-commerce companies were personalizing purchase experiences gave marketers a clue about how to solve the problem of relevance in such a fragmented world of media.

It has become evident that all the preference data caused by media fragmentation, mobile devices, and social media is just the tip of the iceberg of data that can be used for personalization. With the recent craze over smart devices, wearable technology, and the Internet of things, consumers are creating more and more data that tells the world what they do every day, what they like, how much they slept, what they like to eat, where they like to eat it, what they buy, etc. What consumers expect in return is smart, personalized experiences, whether it be in media, applications (e.g., Uber, where we allow the app to monitor our location in return for an easy way to hail a ride), or advertisements.

The big buzzword among CMOs and marketing organizations has been *Big Data*. We have now spent a few years figuring out how to collect all this data. It is time we put it to use in digital advertising to create smart, personalized ad experiences.

4

Data in Advertising

Marketers have used data for probably as long as marketing has existed. Large retailers historically built giant data warehouses of data to analyze consumer behavior and better understand how to market to potential buyers. (The first company I founded, Informatica, now a $1 billion revenue business, sold marketers the software to build these large data warehouses, and my second company, Celequest, which is now part of IBM, built software to help analyze the data.)

Historically data was collected in very large databases and used to do offline analysis of consumer purchase behavior and to plan future marketing spend, based on what was selling, who was buying, etc. Data was crunched to figure out price sensitivity and the impact of sales, coupons, rebates, etc. Much of the data was collected, processed, and used to get a broad understanding of consumer behavior but not in an actionable way to influence consumers to buy.

There are several reasons data was not used in advertising until very recently:

- The data generally represented a single activity that was not actionable. For example, knowing someone bought a case of beer in itself wasn't actionable (unless you simply assume that the person is a beer drinker).

- Data was very siloed. For example, a CRM system had its own data, an email marketing system had its own data, a website had its own data, etc., and tying all of that together on a "common key" was very time-consuming and inaccurate. Therefore, trying to make correlations across data sets was very challenging. This was particularly true between offline data and online data. Offline data may have had keys like last name, address,

Social Security number, etc., while online data may have had either nothing identifiable or things like email address or login information that was difficult to correlate, especially if the online activity occurred outside the brand's properties. For example, while BMW had massive databases of customer data, the company still may not have known or correlated visitors to BMW.com with that data and, similarly, could not correlate it to data from *Car and Driver* for folks reading a review of the latest BMW.

- The data was largely anonymous. Retail purchase data collected by point-of-sale systems had no record of the individual making the purchase. (This is still the case today, except in the case of retailers that have introduced loyalty cards for exactly this reason.)

- Closing the loop to trigger additional purchases had to be done mostly offline (e.g., mailing coupons to the household or sending emails with special offers).

- Data was not very granular. Most data was very broad in its segmentation: It included info on male/female, age, and perhaps purchase behavior but nowhere near the vast amounts of finely segmented detail available now.

- The costs for collecting, processing, and using the data in marketing campaigns were prohibitive, so many marketers just went back to the old "tonnage" method, trying to reach a large number of people with a broad message.

- Concerns about privacy and the activities of privacy advocates prevented marketers from being too aggressive in using customer data. While it is still an issue today, this seems to be waning as a new generation of consumers seem to freely post even their most intimate secrets on social media for the whole world to see. Companies like Facebook and Twitter routinely use this data to serve targeted ads; they figure that because the data was volunteered, it is presumably safe to use.

- Technologies have advanced to a point where it is possible to narrowly identify and segment individuals without actually knowing any personally identifiable information (PII) about them, thus bypassing any privacy concerns. (More on this later.)

Collection and offline analysis of data have had several applications in marketing and are still heavily used by many marketers. Various techniques have been used in trying to determine consumer behavior, ranging from simple reports that show seasonal purchase trends of certain products (e.g., sandwich bags just before school opens) to much more complex "data mining" that produces results like the often-quoted beer-and-diapers correlation. For quite some time, these techniques were viewed as the best marketers could do to determine consumer behavior and market to potential buyers.

Along with the dramatic changes in digital media consumption that accompanied the advent of social media, an important change also occurred in consumer purchasing behavior. The traditional sales funnel, where marketers saw consumers follow a somewhat sequential buying process—often referred to as the "path to purchase"—was no longer being followed by many younger consumers. This change was well documented in the book *Groundswell* by Charlene Li and Josh Bernoff. In this seminal work, they describe the dramatic change occurring in how consumers purchased products and how the Internet and social media had changed the way people went about purchasing products. The book says that a friend's recommendation or posting about a product is more likely to influence a purchase decision than seeing an ad for a product on TV or in a newspaper; the authors found that consumers place less importance on the power of a brand and its recall and instead value research and recommendations from their social networks.

This dramatic change in buying behavior requires a very new approach to collecting and processing data. In fact, even the notion of data itself is changing, with new kinds of data like social media posts, likes, and tweets becoming part of what needs to be analyzed to understand consumer behavior.

With all this data in the hands of advertisers, the question of course becomes "How should the data be used to create more effective advertising?" The first method, which has been used for some time, is targeting. *Targeting* refers to using data to determine whether a user is part of the intended audience segment and only then serving an advertisement to that user.

In the world of TV and print, marketers have tried to achieve targeting by buying media in programming or publications that serve their target audience. So, for example, marketers of outdoor gear may place their ads in *National Geographic* on TV and in print. Similarly, marketers of financial services might target CNBC and CNNMoney.

With digital media, large ad networks and exchanges have inventory or ad impressions covering a wide variety of audience types. Using data management platforms (DMPs), they are able to segment this audience and make it available for purchase by media buyers. For example, you could buy a segment like "auto enthusiasts," which would give you ad impressions only on websites that cater to individuals likely to be interested in automobiles.

Audience segments can be very granular and may even include recent purchase behavior. For example, an audience of "auto intenders" would include people who may have recently browsed auto websites or performed searches for automobiles.

Buying such targeted audiences can be quite expensive because media publishers may have only small numbers of such specialist audiences and so have to sell them at a significant premium over untargeted inventory.

Data targeting also faces a problem in that it is a bit like using a machine gun instead of a rifle: You end up spraying a lot of bullets in hopes of hitting your target instead of making a more focused effort to hit them with precise messaging by intelligently using data you already have.

Audience segments tend to be very broad and general, and so while buying one does make media spend more efficient, the added cost is sometimes not justifiable as you may still be reaching a significant number of people who have no interest whatsoever in the product being marketed.

The additional problem with audience-based targeting is that because most of the data is demographic and behavioral in nature (e.g., age groups, gender, and what websites they visited), this data is simply not sufficient to describe the rather complex path to purchase that emerges with social media and mobile devices playing a big role.

When the word *data* is used in the context of advertising, most people immediately think of data about the consumer or end user. A new type of data is increasingly becoming very relevant to effective personalization of ads. Data about the user's *environment* can also be incredibly valuable in customizing ads to suit users. For example, knowing the local weather where the user is located allows ads to be customized to show products suited for that weather. For example, Starbucks might show a cold iced tea when the weather is 75 degrees or a latte when the weather is below 60 degrees. Awareness of the user's environment is becoming a powerful way to connect with the user because this data is not viewed as personal and therefore does not have any of the typical negative connotations of profile data.

The number of types of data that could be used to personalize advertising has grown significantly over the past few years, primarily due to the proliferation of mobile devices. These devices have really become extensions of ourselves in that they travel with us almost everywhere, except maybe in the shower (though I am sure some have clad their phones in waterproof cases so they can take them into the shower, too). Many activities that we used to conduct on other disconnected devices—like cameras, remote controls, TVs, game consoles, etc.—have all been brought into the palms of our hands in a single device.

Every time you engage with your phone or any of its apps, data has been recorded and probably transmitted to the owner of the app. The app owner can then use the data to serve more personalized content or advertisements, and it can also offer that data up to third parties to create their own content and ad products.

Mobile phones, as it turns out, are again just the tip of the iceberg when it comes to devices we carry around. Fitness trackers, smart connected watches, and other devices are now becoming part of the arsenal of devices we carry around, all of them constantly transmitting data about us to the makers of the devices and applications.

Tying a person to his or her preferences is also starting to get location aware. Many retailers are now testing beacon technology, which can send a coupon or an ad to your mobile device by simply detecting that you are in the vicinity of their store. If you've downloaded the

Starbucks app, you have already seen a bit of this technology in action as it pops up a note every time you get close to a Starbucks shop.

All this points to the fact that data is a strategic asset for marketers and can add significantly to a user's experience and value delivered by the brand by creating unique personalized messages and advertisements that engage users by being relevant and timely.

Brands that embrace data and smartly use it to drive their marketing efforts will leap ahead of their competitors, who still think the best way to get a user engaged is to put a 30-second TV spot in front of them.

5

The Customer Purchase Journey: Increasing Relevance and Engagement

Despite the best efforts in targeting audiences with data and selecting media using all kinds of media analysis and modeling, advertising performance has continued to be challenging. One of the big reasons for this is that the human brain is very adept at ignoring things it does not want to see or absorb.

One of the most impactful books on marketing I have read is *Purple Cow*, by Seth Godin. In this book Godin describes his family driving in the countryside in their car, suddenly coming upon several cows grazing in beautiful pastures. Everyone in the car excitedly gazes out the windows to take a look. Then, a little later, when they see more cows, the reaction is similar. Pretty soon they start seeing hundreds of cows, and they start to ignore the cows and settle back into their seats. Godin asks what would happen if the family suddenly came upon a purple colored cow in the midst of the other cows. Everyone probably would similarly jump out of their seats to take notice, maybe take some pictures, and then they'd probably settle back in if they continue to see more purple cows.

Advertising needs to constantly battle for users' attention. So, when marketers continue to use reach at the lowest costs and "tonnage" as the only tools, they are likely to continuously see lackluster results. The focus needs to shift to ways of increasing relevance and engagement, especially at a time when attention spans are getting shorter and the number of distractions is growing.

I would like to talk about a few key techniques advertisers can use to increase relevance and therefore gain greater engagement with their brands.

The first is to customize and tailor marketing messages to the individual rather than use generic "clever" messaging. Creative agencies spend weeks and months fine-tuning copy and making a single message as broadly appealing as possible, only to find that people simply tune out—likely because the messaging is not relevant to the person viewing the ad.

Due to the constant deluge of information the typical user is bombarded with each day—from various forms of media, chat, email, text messages, social media posts, tweets, etc.—human brains are rapidly evolving to filter material in real time and to process only relevant messaging. The average person receives about 75 emails per day, of which only 42% are important or relevant. It takes about a minute for a user to "recover" and get back in context to the task he or she was conducting before each email shows up.

Consider this: When you gaze at your email, you probably automatically ignore—without even making a conscious decision about it—emails from people you don't think are important, spam, marketing messages, etc. You want to quickly get to the important emails you need to answer. As I was writing this, I glanced at my inbox and saw that I had 72,121 unread emails in my inbox, accumulated over the past 3 years. Clearly, I have managed to get to the emails I need to get to and ignore ones that are (or appear) irrelevant to me.

Advertisements that have messaging tailored to an individual are more likely to get attention and engagement. While tailored messaging is not a revolutionary idea, many marketers have assumed that they can either get away without it or have assumed that it is too difficult to execute such "customized messaging" at scale. Both of these assumptions need to change if a marketer wants results from marketing efforts today.

I recently received two emails which show that brands are starting to see the value and importance of personalization. The first, from Marriott, was an email with a personalized video message custom built just for me: It thanked me for being a loyal Marriott customer and spoke to how many points I had and so on. The second, from Sprint, also contained a video of my statement, with all the details embedded right into the video. These are fine examples of brands showing that they care about my time and speaking directly to me rather than just blasting me with generic messages.

The second key technique for creating engagement is content. Think "content not copy." The idea here is that consumers have become numb to—and largely ignore—broad generic branding messages and copy; they are much more interested in content from a brand that is useful to them. For example, an outdoor biking equipment retailer will have much more luck engaging its audience if it includes videos and other content related to outdoor biking—such as "biking tips for a sunny day" or "mountain biking in 3 easy steps"—rather than generic messages like "Acme bikes—you can ride with us."

The challenge with this content-focused technique is that this content is not easy to distribute. Brands today are starting to spend lots of money generating content for "content marketing," but they're still thinking of content as a silo in itself; this "build it, and they will come" mentality often leads to disappointment. Creating good content is expensive and time-consuming, so why not integrate the content into paid media advertising to make it much more engaging and relevant to users?

The movement toward native advertising formats is really driven by the fact that ads embedded in content and vice versa seem to yield much higher engagement than just ads by themselves.

The third element of creating engagement is timing. I may have seen ads for watches hundreds of times in the past year or so—on TV, in magazines, in newspapers, on websites, in apps, etc.—and yet the time I responded to the ad for a watch was when I was in the market for a new watch, and a watch with exactly the feature I was looking for was delivered to me. If I had seen the ad a week too early or too late, I may not have purchased the watch. On the face of it, this appears to be perhaps the most challenging way to engage users. However, it may not be so challenging if we put some thought into the habits that lead people to purchase. It turns out we actually are pretty good at telling the world when we are ready to buy. For example, we start searching for and browsing the item, we might tell our friends on social media about it, we might take pictures and share them on Instagram or Pinterest. As we get closer to making a decision, we might visit the websites of brands we think may have what we need.

Most of the data trail we leave behind is available instantly to marketers, who can use that information to make sure they get the relevant product advertisement in front of us as quickly as possible.

In the world of automobile purchases, visits to various websites can be indicative of purchase intent. For example, a user visiting the brand's main site may indicate the beginning of interest. If the user then visits Kelley Blue Book's site, chances are she is looking to research car prices and perhaps the trade-in value for her current car. If she browses inventory at a local car dealer, she is seeing if a particular car is available for sale. This is the perfect time to serve a relevant ad to this user. However, in general when to do it is almost impossible to time. What *is* possible is to dynamically track and sequence messaging according to the stage of purchase so that each time the uses sees an ad, she sees content that is more likely to be relevant to where she is in the purchase process.

In the early stages of purchase, where the user is researching, the ads should showcase key features of the car, rich visuals, etc. As the user is exploring costs, perhaps the ads should emphasize special seasonal offers, promotions, etc. When she starts browsing inventory, you can track preferences for color, model, etc., and serve the user ads with inventory for that model, color, etc. Once she has purchased the car, don't stop: Personalize the user's ads with driving tips, ideas for trips, accessories, etc. This is a great time to upsell some accessories.

This kind of intelligent use of data—serving up relevant content and messaging based on data that is available—goes a long way toward increasing engagement.

Matching Personalization to the Customer Path to Purchase

What is the customer journey that leads to purchase? This is an important question for marketers. Traditionally, marketers followed the typical marketing funnel described earlier, where the customer first became aware of the brand, then considered it, then established a preference over other similar brands, and finally purchased it.

Management consulting firms have revised this funnel several times, to factor in the impact of social media and influencers who can sway purchase decisions.

Regardless of the funnel method you believe in or advocate, each stage of the purchase funnel is interested in somewhat different things about the brand. It is also clear that multiple exposures to the brand ultimately lead to purchase. The question, of course, is whether it is simply multiple exposures or multiple exposures with different insights sought and perhaps gained by the buyer that ultimately leads to purchase.

With sequential messaging and personalization of advertisements, the idea is that as the customer progresses through the purchase journey, he may be sharing valuable information about his desires. Smart brands don't just repeat the same broad branding message the user has already seen before; instead, they use this information to customize their messaging to cater to what the customer is likely to want to know next.

Let's consider an automobile purchase cycle. The buyer may have had interest in purchasing an automobile for some time but may not yet be actively looking. At this stage, what is most valuable to her is brand awareness. Given new automobile companies are not created every day, it is not so much about the company brand but about the product brand. It would be useful, for example, to know that Tesla has come out with a family sedan if you were in the market for a family sedan.

Once you have evidence that the buyer has seen a Tesla ad showcasing the new family sedan, showing the same ad again may not achieve much. Perhaps now you should show her an ad that speaks more to the key features of the car, such as the fact that it is electric, luxurious, saves money, etc. If she sees this ad and then actually goes to the Tesla website to browse variations of the car, color, accessories, etc., this is evidence that the user is interested in a car like Tesla. (She may still be comparison shopping, so you cannot conclude that she is ready to buy a Tesla, but you can conclude Tesla is one of her choices.)

The next step for Tesla could be to show a personalized ad with the same preferences of color, style, etc., that the user selected on the website, perhaps with a map to the nearest dealer, maybe even dealer inventory for the model she picked.

If the user does not react to that ad, perhaps she is still comparison shopping, so it may actually be time to put out a financing offer or a special discount package to encourage her to visit the website or a dealership.

Of course buyers don't take a precise path to purchase. Many buyers purchase on visual appeal, others buy because their friends did, still others purchase on technical specifications and features. And, of course, many simply focus on pricing. It is impossible to know up front which camp a prospective buyer falls in. But a lot of data about interests and perhaps even the likely criteria can be gleaned by a good analysis of site visitor data. For example, a buyer who spends a lot of time on the brand's website researching financing options and prices of accessories may be more focused on price, whereas someone who checked out all the engine specs in detail may be more interested in that.

Personalization ideally should be based on real-time data signals. This is really the only way to ensure that a brand can influence a prospective buyer positively before she makes a decision.

Traditionally, data that has been available and used in any kind of personalized marketing has been really stale and is often not actionable in any way. With massive adoption of mobile phones and the apps on them, customers have learned how to procrastinate on purchases because they actually can. Think of how you would book a hotel before you had a smartphone: You either had to go to the hotel's website or call the reservations desk to book a hotel. This meant you had to be at your desk.

Today, you probably are booking your hotel room as you are walking out of the plane after landing at your destination. Due to the amazing apps available that are able to maintain competitive pricing and aggregate hotel availability, procrastinating is not a problem. In fact, it may even be rewarding. I discovered, for example, that many airlines and hotels have started steeply discounting their seats and rooms in the hours before they become useless.

An airplane seat yields no revenue if it is empty when the plane takes off. Likewise, the later in the evening it gets for a hotel with empty rooms, the less likely it is that all the rooms will get filled. Selling a room or an airplane seat for even half off can yield revenue and avoid a loss on that seat or room.

Similarly, new apps are available that are arbitraging restaurant reservations the day before or the same day because of cancellations. They're offering up those newly available seats to folks who may have been waiting for them but couldn't get in because the restaurants have been booked.

This tells us that data has a significant time value in today's market. Personalized advertising that can take advantage of events and data occurring "in the moment" can significantly increase engagement and sales for a brand.

The customer journey to purchase has become increasingly unpredictable and is often influenced by events happening around the customer. Mobile technology has also made it possible for customers to execute purchases "in the moment," without a lot of planning or thinking, just because the right offer or product is offered to them at the right time.

This completely throws off a lot of the traditional thinking about the path or journey to purchase. It is no longer sequential, timed, or predictable. It is critical for brands to understand this well and be prepared to appear at various moments in a customer's daily life— educating, entertaining, building a relationship, and hopefully being the last point of influence before a purchase is executed. This is really the only way brands in this new world can ensure success.

The new reality doesn't require just an incremental change or adjustment in thinking. Rather, it calls for a very different mindset that puts consumers first and arguably in the driver's seat, as they share with brands their preferences and allow brands to provide them what they need to make sound decisions to purchase. The era of talking down to consumers and blasting irrelevant messages and constantly interrupting them with the same ineffective advertisement will only serve to alienate this new kind of buyer. Incidentally, these buyers also have all their choices in their hands via their increasingly more powerful smartphones and apps; a brand's competition is literally just an app or a tap away.

Personalized advertising is about changing the way we market to individuals. It is not as much trying to predict and follow the customer purchase journey as trying to always be at the right place at the right time—ideally at the point where the customer is making a purchase decision. It does away with the linear process of thinking and with the idea of mass marketing, and it aims to get precision and relevance and to create the kind of engagement that will deliver results.

6

Targeting vs. Personalization

Targeting is a word every advertising practitioner had at the tip of his tongue a few years ago. Targeting came about as a solution to the media fragmentation problem described earlier.

As media became increasingly fragmented, it was becoming very difficult for brands and media-buying agencies to buy the kinds of media they know would actually reach their audience. There was really no scalable way to find even a few million people on the Internet who belonged to an audience segment like "gardening enthusiasts."

To solve this problem, advertising networks began aggregating vast amounts of such inventory to make it easier for media agencies to buy inventory from a single source rather than many different individual publishers. This solved the aggregation problem but created a new one: It was impossible for brands to know if they were indeed reaching their audience.

Ad networks quickly offered a solution in the form of "targeted audience buying," where using largely behavioral data (i.e., knowing what sites people frequented), they were able to categorize their inventory into "audiences" that brands could purchase.

Targeted audience buying was a fad for a while, but marketers soon realized that not only did they have to pay significantly higher premiums for any form of targeting, but also there was no way of verifying that they were actually reaching their target audience. In fact, in many cases, there wasn't even a way of verifying that they were reaching an audience of people rather than robots and fake traffic on ad networks. Brands therefore resorted to what could probably best described as "spray and pray": They would buy large amounts of untargeted inventory at the lowest possible price and deliver as many ad impressions as possible. (Sound familiar?)

If broad bands of audience targeting like "males between 20 and 40" and "females between 30 and 50" were specified in media RFPs, it was almost the same as not having any targeting at all, given that there wasn't any real way to verify or confirm this. It is also not clear that such broad targeting parameters actually cause any improvements in performance over nontargeted media. From an ROI standpoint, you just end up paying more to reach a smaller number of people.

One of the reasons such "audience buying" simply did not work is that it was based on ad networks and exchanges classifying websites into audience bands. This wasn't terribly scientific but was simply based on the opinion of the individual doing the allocation. Some of the audience measurement tools, like Comscore and Nielsen, tried to provide some validation of these claims, but again, the bands were very broad and did little to help deliver messages to narrowly targeted audiences.

Programmatic media-buying platforms and data management platforms (DMPs) made this somewhat better because software represented the type of audience segment being delivered. Also, because the DMPs were independent of the media sellers, presumably there was some semblance of verification and a lot more than just the media seller's promise that the brand was indeed reaching the targeted audience.

Overall, while targeting has brought some ability for brands to try to reach their audiences, more accurately it really has been a lot of "throw something out there and see what sticks" rather than more precise messaging and tailored content and creativity that creates engagement with audiences.

Personalization that involves tailoring messaging using data about the user the advertisement is being delivered to is far more effective than just throwing a broad message out there and hoping it is relevant to someone.

Data-driven personalization without a doubt also comes with costs. However, the costs are usually in the form of increments to ad serving costs rather than media costs. With ad serving costs typically less than 10% of the associated media costs, I am sure most marketers can quickly do the math and see that from an ROI perspective, they are better off buying lightly targeted media and using personalization to ensure that the relevant audiences are getting targeted messages.

Another term usually used for personalization is *micro-targeting*. Media targeting often cannot get very narrow. Most publishers prefer to sell undifferentiated inventory because fragmenting their inventory into narrow audience segments usually creates massive issues with fill rates or inability to deliver on campaigns if they don't segment off the inventory exclusively for use with a particular segment.

Because personalization is not really dependent on media but rather on external sources of data that tell us a person's interests and what audience segments he belongs to, it is possible to very narrowly target messaging—almost down to an individual.

Targeting also does not really solve the problem of user apathy to advertisements. This is a big issue and the reason behind the lackluster performance of digital advertising. In an attempt to ensure that a message is relevant to a broad audience, marketing teams often come up with messaging that is bland and uninteresting. This "one-size-fits-all" messaging is often designed to appeal to everyone but usually ends up appealing to no one.

Re-targeting, which has become very successful in recent years, is essentially targeting taking a big turn toward personalization. If you think about it, re-targeting is very different from targeting. Targeting is directed at people we are guessing may be interested in a product, based on their age, gender, where they live, etc. Re-targeting, on the other hand, uses hard factual data that someone actually visited a brand's website and stated interest very clearly to the brand. So, in essence, re-targeting (the unfortunate name notwithstanding) is much more about personalization than about targeting. Indeed, most personalization projects start with website activity as a primary source of data to personalize an ad.

Using just targeting is a missed opportunity when it comes to engaging with users. It is hard enough to get someone's attention with a brand's advertisement among all the clutter of content and distractions of media, email, texts, tweets, posts, etc. But can you really blame users for ignoring your advertisements when you have nothing interesting to say to them? Why not make your messages stand out and be relevant?

7

Native Advertising, Content Marketing, and Personalization

Native advertising and content marketing, while entirely different ways of advertising, have a lot in common with and are sometimes confused with personalized advertising, and so it is worth discussing them a bit.

For large brands, understanding the synergies between their content marketing, native advertising, and personalized advertising initiatives can also avoid duplication of efforts and enable the teams working on these initiatives to collaborate and share resources rather than work in silos, duplicating efforts and wasting resources.

Native advertising has many definitions but perhaps one thing we can all agree on is that it is advertising designed to fit in well and perhaps even blend into the content of a site. Another way to look at a native ad is as an ad that is personalized to a site. Indeed, many native ad platforms "borrow" the style sheets and look and feel of the hosting site in order to mimic the look and feel of the site. Such platforms are also integrated into the CMS of the site to pull in site content to customize the ad. So, in many ways, architecturally native ads are similar to personalized ads but perhaps with much simpler data and content integration requirements since they are personalized to a site rather than to a person.

Native ads have a lot in common with personalized ads in that the content of a native ad is fluid and dynamically populated, much like a personalized ad. Where they differ is in the depth and breadth of data used to drive the creative content to be displayed and in the sophistication of the rules and optimizations involved in delivering personalized advertising campaigns. In general, a personalized ad serving platform can be used to deliver native ads but not vice versa.

Content marketing has taken hold in a big way in most marketing organizations. Content marketing—sometimes also referred to as *earned media*—can drive engagement with a brand without a lot of the associated media costs. The earliest form of content marketing was probably YouTube videos; brands could upload videos in the style of user-generated video content and hope that it would get shared and viewed. More recently, social media platforms created entirely around the idea of sharing content have become very important platforms for content marketing efforts.

Given the importance of this earned media model, brands have set up teams within their marketing organizations or agencies to focus on developing content that is to be shared in social media platforms, which seem to be growing each day. Facebook, Twitter, Instagram, Pinterest, Vine, and other social media sites are becoming very scalable platforms for distributing branded content to large numbers of users. Such models now are also incorporating paid media models to extend the reach of the content.

Content marketing and personalized advertising have a lot in common because they are both focused on the idea of presenting relevant content to users and doing so in a timely and dynamic manner more akin to publishing than broadcasting. Where they differ is that personalized advertising is armed with data about the user, which makes the content much more targeted and relevant to the user because it is tailored to the user. Content marketing within social media is starting to offer such models, using a social media platform's own data. So within social media platforms, content marketing and personalized advertising in some ways are blending together in such a manner that they may eventually be indistinguishable.

Several publishers have integrated content marketing into their paid media offerings to create "native ads at scale" products. Notably, Federated Media has a set of "conversationalist" units that integrate site content with ad copy and deliver the result both as content-well ad units (which are in the content stream of sites) and as display ad units, which provide scale as they can be served in display ad inventory. Blogher, an aggregator of women's content sites (which recently merged with SheKnows), also has some ad formats that combine native content in display units.

In the world outside social media, content marketing and personalized advertising are very distinct and are often executed by different teams within a brand or an agency. Terms like *content at scale* have been coined in reference to the inherent lack of scale within social media platforms for earned media and in reference to the fact that with paid media, content marketing models can achieve scale.

The clear line of distinction ultimately between native advertising, content marketing and other such disciplines, and personalized advertising is that personalized advertising—as the name implies—is centered on the person. It uses data in as many forms and from as many places as possible to create a unique and personalized experience for the end user. The content, media, and other aspects of personalized advertising are secondary; the primary goal of personalized advertising is to ensure that a user sees what is relevant to him or her and hopefully engages with the brand as a result.

It is quite possible that, over time, all these different disciplines will blend together to become one thing. If I were to bet, it would be about personalized advertising as it is much more accountable and scalable, and it puts the most important person, the customer, in the center.

8

Dynamic Creative Optimization
vs. Personalization

The earliest forms of dynamic creative and messaging were very simplistic in nature. A brand would come up with a few alternative creative and messaging formats and then serve the ads to a target audience and then use the results to pick the messaging that was yielding the best results in terms of user engagement. This technique, referred to as dynamic creative optimization (DCO), has been used for some time. Technology platforms developed for this purpose have been around for quite a while, and most of them are now part of larger companies. For example, Teracent is now part of Google, Tumri is now part of Collective Media, and Dapper is now part of Yahoo.

While DCO was a great first attempt at customizing and optimizing creative and messaging to users, it didn't really take advantage of the wealth of data now available to drive such customization of messaging at scale.

DCO originated in performance marketing and direct response campaigns where advertisers measured the successful outcomes of campaigns based on the number of people who clicked on an ad and the number of "conversions" (i.e., purchases completed by people who saw or engaged with the ad).

Measurement for such campaigns was rooted in ensuring the lowest possible cost for a campaign because the goal was to produce the highest number of conversions for a given cost. This drive to reduce the cost of conversion meant that use of data and other dynamic ad technologies was minimal as it was hard to justify the additional costs of the data and technology relative to the ROI.

Recently, with data becoming more freely available at a fine enough grain to be valuable for personalizing ads, data has become a key element of dynamic advertising.

Early improvements on creative optimization included using cookie data from a site to personalize an ad. For example, if you went to a clothing retailer's website and looked at a dress, in a particular color or style, a cookie could be used to record those preferences, and instead of showing you a generic ad for the clothing retailer, it would show you exactly that dress and perhaps even suggestions of similar dresses that you might like or a pairing of the dress with some nice shoes, etc.

The idea of using data—primarily profile data, such as from DMP platforms and real-time data gathered from a user's environment to create a more engaging ad experience—is the next level to which dynamic creative can go.

Using a cookie for personalization of an ad is a neat idea but ignores the millions who never went to the retailer's website and therefore are served generic ads that they largely ignore.

With DCO, the focus has been significantly more on optimization. It has been all about trying to figure out which of many creative alternatives a user is likely to engage with. Some of these alternatives may be somewhat smart—such as whether users are likely to respond to a special discount offer on price or to nice visuals of a car. The more mundane alternatives may be experimenting with color of the creative elements, messaging like "Special offer" vs. "Reduced prices," etc.

Several DCO platforms also tout algorithms that can take in various creative variations and weight them based on engagement metrics, trying of course to figure out which variations of messaging, images, or video would produce the best results.

The challenge in general with DCO has been that it has involved throwing a lot out in front of consumers and trying to see what sticks. A much better approach has emerged that instead tries to better understand the individual user's likes and dislikes and to deliver intelligently tailored creative and messaging to them. This is what personalized advertising is all about.

The focus and emphasis in personalized advertising are on the data and rules and algorithms applied to the data to determine the best messaging and creative personalized to the individual. Some examples are knowing when the weather is warm in an area so Dunkin' Donuts can market cold drinks instead of hot coffee, knowing a user frequently travels to a destination and selecting hotel or airline offers at that destination, knowing the individual is a sports enthusiast and tying a drink to celebrating a sporting event with that drink, etc.

Personalization of ads is also attracting brand-building marketers who see it as a way of creating brand awareness and engagement, using data to customize the content and messaging in the ad to a particular individual.

DCO platforms often are not very well suited to delivering personalized advertisements. The reason is that with personalized advertising, the emphasis is less on serving the creative and measuring outcomes but rather on data signals and rules—areas in which most DCO platforms are weak. Integration of the creative itself to these rules and data is critical to achieve scale with personalized advertising.

While DCO was a great start to the idea of dynamic advertising, it is the addition of data to figure out the right messaging to an individual that is a game changer when it comes to creating user engagement.

9

Twitter Comes to Display Advertising

In addition to the abundance of very fine-grained data about users, social media platforms like Facebook and Twitter have introduced an entirely new way of advertising "in the moment."

Facebook and Twitter (soon to be joined by other social media platforms) have completely changed the model of traditional media planning and execution. In traditional advertising models, a brand started with a big concept/idea and then spent weeks or even months with a creative agency, ideating and brainstorming various messaging, clever quips, catchy jingles, etc. This then went into an equally lengthy and cumbersome media planning process, where media was selected and negotiated, and then there was a rather arduous process of creative production and campaign launch, which often took weeks or months as well.

All this planning and work meant that brands could never really take advantage of things that users are thinking about and responding to. For example, it was impossible to engage users with messaging around a celebrity's shaving his or her head. Brands also struggle with being able to participate or support something like the ice-bucket challenge for ALS that became popular in 2014. This is due to the longer planning and creative cycles needed to launch campaigns.

Twitter and Facebook are providing platforms to reach audiences in real time with relevant messaging around what they are thinking about. Witness, for example, the Oreos "you can still dunk in the dark" tweet during the power outage at the 2013 Super Bowl. This was perfectly timed and generated 15,000 retweets within minutes of the original tweet.

The candy bar brand Kit Kat capitalized on "Bendgate" when the iPhone 6 came out, and users reported that the phone would bend if kept in a jeans pocket. Kit Kat tweeted an image of a broken candy bar with the caption "We don't bend, we #break. #bendgate #iPhone6 plus." This tweet was retweeted more than 28,000 times in a very short while.

The number of retweets of each of these advertisements shows how powerful delivering the right message at the right time can be. Considering these were unpaid media campaigns, the results are quite phenomenal.

While Twitter, Facebook, and other social media platforms tout similar examples of how powerful personalized, or "in the moment," marketing can be, there are several challenges with this approach. First, ad formats on Twitter and Facebook are very limited. While Facebook and Twitter are continuing to evolve their ad formats, concerns about upsetting users have kept them from really being able to offer the kinds of creative experiences that other media offer.

Second—and importantly—as successful as these campaigns were, they received retweets and likes in the tens of thousands, which is hardly the kind of scale that brands look for, especially considering that most tweets from brands get hardly any engagement due to the reliance on users to spread the word. Still, such successes offer excellent ROI considering that the media cost is zero.

So, in general, catching people in the moment seems like a great idea, but doing so at scale requires applying the techniques and technology platforms capable of delivering personalized advertising. There is no exact science to creating witty and creative campaigns, and so they are very hard to replicate, especially when campaigns need to deliver hard ROI to marketers who are constantly being evaluated on how they impact sales.

A very powerful combination is the scale and reach of display advertising and the relevance and in-the-moment capabilities of Twitter and Facebook to deliver dynamic, personalized advertising at scale. Such an approach fundamentally changes the way a campaign cycle should be viewed. The traditional process of launching a campaign was a very linear process, somewhat along these lines:

Create Idea/Concept → Plan Media → Develop Creative Assets
→ Produce Ad → Launch Campaign → Measure → Optimize

Today's world of real-time messaging in social media, large amounts of data to personalize ads, and technology to deliver such personalized messaging at scale requires a different process. This new process needs to look a lot more like the process shown in Figure 9.1.

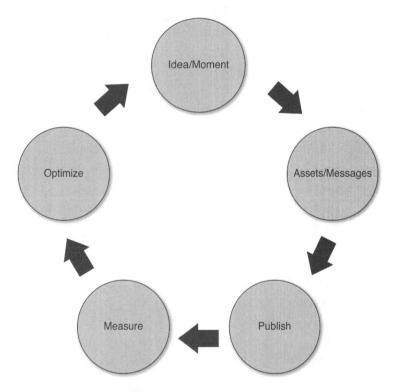

Figure 9.1 New process for personalized advertising

The idea here is that marketing and advertising become not a discrete set of "campaigns" but rather a continuous dialogue and communication between brands and their customers and prospective customers. Whether the campaign is for a telco company that is very focused on pricing and offers or deals or a luxury brand that needs to be perceived as "in the know" about key luxury trends, this concept of real-time messaging and marketing in the moment is key.

For a luxury watch brand, for example, the messaging may change based on the calendar (e.g., "Buy your valentine a watch," "Be a generous Santa, give her time"), on events (e.g., "Wear a Michele to your Oscar party" or "Clooney just got married, check out what he's wearing"), or on other things that may be happening at that very moment.

For a pricing-driven telco, when a competitor comes up with a new discount offer on a data plan, the brand needs to respond immediately, swapping out messaging with a new offer. Or if there was a delay in the launch of a new product from a competitor, the brand might capitalize on it by saying "Why wait?" This was something Samsung brilliantly did as a counter move when Apple was getting a lot of PR for the fact that people were waiting in line at Apple stores, hoping—often in vain—that they could get their hands on an iPhone. Samsung came out with an ad showing Apple customers waiting in line and people walking by with a Samsung phone that looked much like an iPhone, touting the message "you can have it now" and making fun of the folks waiting in line for an Apple phone.

For almost every brand, several moments present unique opportunities to communicate with customers and prospects and try to get them engaged somehow. This has been the dream of many marketers. It has not been until recently that sufficient amounts of detailed data, timely information about what is going on (via social media), and technology to deliver such personalized messaging at scale have become available. All these factors add up to a tremendous opportunity for brands to get engaged with their audiences in meaningful ways and drive loyalty and sales.

10

Data, Events, and Rules

The idea of personalized advertising is really about combining three things: data about individual preferences or their environment, rules and algorithms to process this data and determine what messages and creative elements to show an individual, and measurement of engagement outcomes to enable further optimization of the rules and algorithms.

Data Signals and Events

Today we have significantly more kinds and sources of data and event "triggers" that can be used to deliver targeted and customized creative and messaging to consumers:

- **Profile data:** Profile data includes data about users and the audience segments they belong to, such as males, females, age groups, purchasing habits, income, household metrics, etc.
- **CRM data:** CRM data refers to data that brands usually record and store in customer relationship management software systems or databases when you directly interact with them; for example, purchasing or registering a product.
- **Environmental data:** Data about the environment the user is in can be determined in real time and used to deliver tailored messaging. Examples include local weather, temperature, geographic location, time of the day, or day of the week (e.g., "TGIF, go home and have a Bud").
- **Real-time events:** Other events that are occurring at the time—such as sporting events (e.g., Super Bowl, U.S. Open,

World Cup Soccer) or entertainment events (e.g., Grammys, Oscars)—can be triggers.

- **Social media data:** Data about users' actions within social media as well as style or fashion trends can be triggers, as can news and topics being discussed (e.g., the tan suit President Obama was wearing, the Gangnam style phenomenon).

- **Site/cookie data:** First-party cookies on consumer websites for product-based retargeting can be triggers.

- **Search data:** This refers to data obtained when users search for items or interests. Search data can be a very powerful source of personalization data because it is indicative of interest and perhaps even timing of a purchase.

- **Contextual data:** This refers to data about where an ad is being viewed; for example, what section of a website.

Profile Data

Thanks to profile data, multi-brand marketers may use a single campaign and media buy to ensure focused messaging to specific audience segments within the media buy.

For example, an auto manufacturer like Mercedes could use profile data to show the Mercedes GL, a high-end SUV, to moms who live in higher-net-worth geographies while showing the entry-level CLA cars to younger males who are more likely buyers of the CLA.

Profile data could also be used to message different aspects of a car to different audience segments. For example, men might respond better to messaging about the ruggedness of a car in mountain terrain and specs of the engine, while women may respond better to messaging about cargo space, safety, etc. This kind of micro-messaging can be as fine-grained as the data itself. For example, BMW owners could receive messaging about how a Mercedes costs less to own than a BMW or may receive offers of special upgrade packages. Auto intenders or individuals who recently browsed auto comparison sites or searched for trade-in pricing could be given special offers.

Another example of the use of profile data to target messaging is cable companies offering programming packages. For example, an ad campaign promoting different sporting packages like soccer, baseball, tennis, etc., could dynamically deliver messaging relative to the demographic signals to determine the packages to message in an ad. For example, Hispanic and European populations are likely to be good targets for marketing soccer packages.

For consumers, this kind of micro-messaging is much more valuable than broad messaging or even wrong messaging. From a media efficiency standpoint, this kind of micro-messaging can produce very significant media ROI because untargeted media can be purchased programmatically by media teams and used to deliver very fine-grained messaging to individual audience segments.

The cost economics usually work well because targeted media often ends up adding as much as 30% to 40% to the average CPM fees for media. Compared to the often less than 5% cost of data profiles, this nets out to very significant savings for media buying. Because targeted media is usually sold in very broad audience segments compared to the granularity with which data can be purchased, the net effect is that significantly higher engagement can be achieved via micro-messaging within a broad audience.

CRM Data

A broader set of profile data is available to brands that have a direct relationship with their customers. This is especially true for brands that offer products directly from their websites and/or their branded retail outlets. The data in these cases is much richer and detailed, including things like purchase history, loyalty, average purchase amounts, and even demographics and wealth brackets. Online-only retailers, of course, like Zappos, eBay, drugstore.com, Amazon, and others, have vast amounts of this CRM data.

The challenge with CRM data has typically been that in most organizations, integrating CRM data with advertising is pretty challenging due to a host of technical and political issues. For example, such profile data often belongs to the operations team and is managed by corporate IT. It can often be a long and difficult process for the marketing team to gain access to the data. Many companies are also thinking through the privacy implications of using such data in personalizing advertisements and clearly want to be careful not to be viewed as profiting from the trust relationship they have with customers.

How CRM data is used can vary by industry, too. For example, Amazon and FreshDirect have been running banner advertisements personalized with preferences of their customers. This makes sense because if you are on a gluten-free diet, it is useful for FreshDirect to showcase gluten-free products in ads delivered to you. On the other hand, brands like Charles Schwab need to be careful as an ad personalized to you may reveal the kinds of investment products you own or your net worth—things you don't necessarily want your colleagues to know about if you have the personalized Schwab ad on a website pulled up at work. A more extreme example would be drugstore.com showing ads with a drug for a psychiatric condition that folks may not know you have.

Despite the possible problems, the use of CRM data in advertisements is growing by leaps and bounds. Most marketing teams have funded large Big Data projects centered around using data they already have to better target and personalize their advertising.

The increase in the use of CRM data also coincides with a shift in consumer attitudes about privacy. People seem to increasingly understand the trade-off between the value of personalization and the impact on privacy of their data.

In the end, whether or not CRM data should be used for advertising will be a choice each brand has to make. When a company does choose to use it, good judgment should be applied in using such data.

Environmental Data

Geographic data can be used to deliver very effective engagement by customizing an ad for local audiences. For example, auto companies used to have to go through the very cumbersome process of allocating co-op marketing funds and managing creative integrity across large dealerships across the country. Today they can simply enable ads to dynamically display creative messaging customized for each local market.

An advertisement could, for example, show the local dealer's name, phone number, and other details, as well as inventory of cars available at the dealer and pricing.

Geographically enhanced ads are especially effective with the significant adoption and use of mobile devices. An ad showing local information will be significantly more likely to result in the user visiting the dealership than will an ad with generic brand messaging.

Geographic data can also be used to customize and blend in a localized feel for the brand. For example, seaside residents could be shown the car ad with beach images, while mountainside residents could be shown imagery related to mountains.

Using weather data combined with geographic data is also a powerful way to customize an ad and its messaging. For example, Jack Daniels Honey recently ran a campaign where multiple creative showed various Jack Daniels drinks and cocktails, while the skin of the ad showed different local weather conditions. The ads related to users' environments, and the campaign was very effective at having users relate to the ads.

Several brands, like banking brands, use various images of ethnically diverse talent in their ads. These ads can be much more effective if they are programmed with geographic information. For example, they can show Hispanic talent much more in the south of the country, Asian talent in San Francisco, and a very diverse rotation of talent in major metropolitan cities.

Real-Time Events

The idea of relating marketing messages to events happening in real time originated in social media like Facebook. Twitter, Vine, Snapchat, Instagram, and others have taken the idea further by allowing brands to message directly to consumers.

For brands working with display advertising, the same kind of real-time or event-driven messaging can also be incorporated into display campaigns. Creative for display advertising can now be dynamically changed in real time, as events are occurring.

Sporting events, major entertainment events, and even national news can be used to customize ad experiences dynamically.

For example, in the San Francisco Bay area, where there are a lot of 49ers and Giants fans, the messaging of the ad before a game could be changed to say "Go 49ers; good luck Monday" or "Fear the beard."

There are, in general, two kinds of event-based dynamic ads. First, preprogrammed ads are suited for events that are known and scheduled ahead of time, such as football games or the Grammys. These events are easy to manage in advertising campaigns because the creative and copy to be displayed can be determined and approved ahead of time. These kinds of events can be programmed into the dynamic advertising platform, and once the campaign is in flight, the creative will change in response to the schedule setup.

The second type of event-based dynamic ads is real-time ads. Real-time event-based advertising has primarily been in the realm of social media, particularly Twitter, because the real-time messaging nature of Twitter fits well with the idea of real-time "sponsored tweets" or other kinds of messaging that leverages data about the user to tailor messaging to the user.

The main challenge with Twitter, Facebook, and other social media platforms, of course, is the very limited ad formats they are able to offer if they want to avoid upsetting users. The kinds of large, rich storytelling ad formats that big brands like are hard to accomplish in social media platforms. This is one of the biggest reasons real-time advertising ideas are quickly transferring from social media to mainstream display advertising.

The ad agency Universal McCann launched an initiative called "moments marketing." The idea behind moments marketing is to use data and events occurring at a given moment to customize creative and messaging to each user (see Figure 10.1). Paired with programmatic media, this creates a scalable way to engage users with targeted messaging.

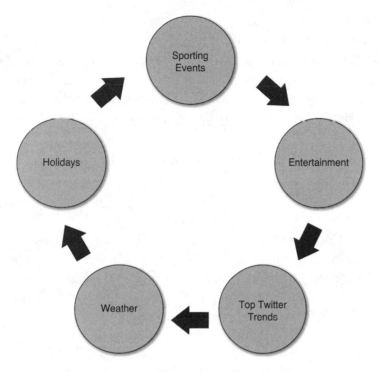

Figure 10.1 Example of data signals in a moments marketing campaign

Social Media Data

Social media data can reveal a lot about a person's interests and is a very rich source of data for personalized advertising. While advertising within a social media platform, this data is somewhat readily available. Most social media platforms offer various targeting segments that an advertiser can use to more precisely target its messaging.

Social media platforms often allow advertisers to pick interests (for example, sports fans), demographics (for example, single men), as well as friends of fans (who may likely have similar interests), and so on.

Outside the social media platforms, a variety of methods and techniques exist to use this data to personalize advertisements. Many social media applications that users have accepted are able to get (depending on the permissions the users allow the app) information about the user. For example, an app that shows you all the places you have traveled can of course use that data to personalize advertising.

Fans or followers of a brand can also be targeted by those brands to post messages to their social media news feeds.

It is likely social media platforms will also start offering this data on their audience networks, which is where they essentially allow advertisers to buy media on other sites and mobile applications and can use their data to more precisely target and personalize the ads to those users.

Certain vendors and media networks have offered targeted advertising based on so-called social signals. It is not clear, however, how much reach and accuracy these signals have within the target audience for a brand.

The other kind of social media data that is also useful to advertisers in understanding what's on their audience's mind is to tap into social media trends. Most social media platforms publish a daily or sometimes real-time set of trending topics; this reflects in a broad sense what the chatter on social media is mostly about and can be tapped by brands to have a greater likelihood of being relevant and in the moment. The biggest benefit of this approach is that the data is freely available and is even available on a regional and local basis for more precise messaging; for example, most of the folks in San Francisco might be thinking about a 49ers game on game day, while their counterparts in Boston may be thinking about a Red Sox game if there happens to be one on that same day.

Site/Cookie Data

As users browse websites, they are essentially indicating their preferences and likes in an indirect way. For example, users visiting the Car and Driver site would select the kinds of cars they are likely to be in the market for. In some cases, consumption of content on a site does not directly correlate to purchase intent. For example, very few people who read reviews of the latest Ferrari are likely to buy that car. Nevertheless, site data can provide very important insights into consumer interest and intent.

Several startup companies have recently introduced personalization software for websites. The idea is that rather than a website being static and one-size-fits-all, the site gets dynamically configured for the user, based on a continuous process of learning about the consumer's interests.

The idea of using site data to personalize site content is about as old as websites themselves. During the dot-com boom, personalization was all the rage for e-commerce sites. Amazon, of course, was the king of personalization, using its recommendation technology.

E-commerce sites constantly record what products you are browsing on the site and then use vast amounts of consumer data from the site to make correlations between what you browsed for and what you are likely to be interested in as a result. The kinds of predictions and correlations can range from the very simple and direct to patterns that can get very complex and intelligent, all using data volunteered by you. Here are some examples of assumptions that companies might make based on browsing patterns:

- People who buy a printer are likely to need ink cartridges in three months.
- People who shop for diapers are likely to shop for sippy cups, washcloths, and baby clothing.
- People who shop for expensive cameras may also be in the market for tablets and other expensive gadgets.
- People who booked an air ticket to a warm location are likely to shop for swimwear.

When such recommendation technologies first came out, they were very focused on targeting consumers within the site to encourage them to purchase more from the site. Such technologies are now rapidly expanding outside the site. They are being used to deliver highly personalized interest- and intent-based ads to those same consumers well after they have left the site.

As an example of how this would work, imagine that a user goes to an automobile website and browses for a car. She is essentially demonstrating interests in the model type, price range, preowned or new, color, features, etc. This data is probably recorded in a cookie that is placed on the user's computer. An advertising campaign for that brand can now be dynamically configured to read the information in the cookie and personalize the ad with the car model, price, and color the user browsed.

This type of personalization can be used for almost any brand that has such user preferences and interests. The important thing to note here is that while this concept originated on e-commerce sites, it can be extended to any consumer product or even business-to-business site. For example, anyone reviewing Cisco's products on the Cisco website can be retargeted with ads that showcase products the user showed interest in.

By using product catalog feeds that are available on many e-commerce sites, this concept could be extended to showcase a whole subcatalog of products customized to the user, maybe in combination with weather and other data signals.

Search Data

Search data is the hardest type of data to come by. Since Google switched to secure search, which hides the referrer URL's search term, it has become impossible to use a search term to personalize ads on a site. However, some data providers (e.g., DMPs) do provide aggregated search data (e.g., using site-specific searches) that can be used to customize advertisements. Specific publishers also make available search results that can be accessed by an advertisement to personalize the ad.

Search data is very personal and should be used with a lot of caution as it can directly reveal things about the users that they may not want others to know about.

Contextual Data

Most media publisher sites have various sections that may have different kinds of context. For example, many news sites (e.g., CNN, USA Today) have sections for sports, finance, lifestyle, etc. Often a media purchase is done for the whole site and run on all pages. However, it is also possible to have dynamic personalization of an ad, based on the section or context in which it is running. For example, messaging for an alcohol brand might refer to tailgating in the sports section, celebrating an up day in the market or drowning your sorrows on a down day in the market in the financial section, etc.

Such contextually driven personalized ads can be very effective at creating customized messaging for the audience profile of visitors to a specific section of the publisher's site and can be done without creating a lot of complexity in terms of individual ads and ad tags.

Combining Data Signals

One of the great things about a data-driven approach to personalization is that a more holistic picture of the individual can be drawn through the intelligent use of multiple sources of data.

Remember our earlier automobile example involving using site data to customize the ad experience? We could also combine that data with profile data from a DMP to, for example, deliver messaging that is gender specific, for example saying "The perfect SUV to take the family skiing this weekend" vs. "The perfect SUV to take the kids to soccer."

An even more compelling example would be a clothing retailer using gender data to customize an ad to show clothing relevant to the user by combining product interest data with gender data. This is particularly useful and important when the individual did not visit the website at all. Use of various data signals also helps close gaps in data where one data source may not have information at all about an individual, whereas another could have the information that would be just as useful for personalization.

Combining various data signals to create an intelligent and personalized ad enables advertisers to shed the stigmas usually associated with retargeting and use of profile data.

New Forms of Data

As use of personal devices like smartphones and tablets is growing exponentially, so is the amount of data being collected and made available for personalized advertising. Smartphones and tablets alone are generating petabytes of data on each user as he or she consumes media and uses various apps.

Wearable devices (e.g., FitBit and other fitness devices, smart watches) are collecting even more data than smartphones and tablets, and the data they are collecting is even more personal than what smart-phones and tables are gathering. For example, fitness devices know when you went to bed, when you woke up, how much you worked out, how many steps you walked, etc. (Not to be outdone, the new iPhone 6 has its own health app built in to collect such data.)

Without a doubt, all this data isn't being collected to personalize advertising but to provide functionality in the app or device. It opens up opportunities for marketers to better understand the users they are marketing to and ensure that they are delivering messages and building awareness of their products in an intelligent manner.

With more personal data, of course, marketers have to be very careful about how it is used. For a user, there is a fine line between viewing personalization as value being provided by the brand and feeling like the brand is abusing the user's trust and the personal information it has access to.

Several retailers and hotel chains are experimenting with beacon technology, which allows them to serve up coupons or ads to mobile devices of customers, based on data about those users. This is just the beginning of where personalization crosses device boundaries and can become a combination of location, environment, context, and profile of an individual.

Beacons themselves just provide an identifier of a location and brand/product. However, because the beacon receiver is embedded in a mobile app, advertisements that are much more personalized to the user can be delivered based on which area of the retail store the user is browsing as well as any personal preference data available to the app. For example, a beacon may just identify that a user is in the electronics aisle at a Target store, but the Target or other shopping app will then be able to pop up an advertisement with an offer related to a blender that perhaps the user browsed for a few days ago on Target.com.

Here again, popping up an ad/offer every five minutes when a user is in or near a retail store may create a negative feeling toward the brand. In fact, early research shows that mobile apps that constantly interrupt with offers lose usage very significantly, as the users just simply turn off the apps.

Beacon technology is showing a lot of promise in tracking conversions (that is, sales that can be attributed to online advertising). There is also a lot of potential to use beacons to do forms of retargeting. However, beacon-enabled mobile applications at this time still do not provide the kind of scale to be effective for most brands. This is bound to change as more and more applications become beacon enabled.

Rules and Matching

Rules and algorithms are necessary to ensure that a data signal is interpreted correctly in order to determine the conditions under which a particular message should be delivered.

There are generally two kinds of rules used for matching data signals to determine what messaging or creative assets should be displayed in an ad: direct index (DI) and a dynamic rule.

A DI is a value that is calculated or looked up in order to create a mapping between a data signal and assets designated for that particular user or group of users. A DI is ideal when there are thousands or even hundreds of thousands of user profiles to be mapped to assets and messaging. It is also often used when there is a simple and direct mapping possible between a data signal and the messaging assets. For example, a retailer may have product identifiers being used for retargeting users. In this case, the product identifier in the cookie will map directly to a specific product, such as Nike LunarGlide shoes. With a DI, the matching is very simple: It is a simple and direct match between the data signal/user or segment identifier and the messaging assets to be delivered.

A more complex kind of matching, often referred to as a dynamic rule, is often required for one of the following reasons:

- A range may need to be established. If the data signal is temperature, it may be necessary to define a temperature range to determine the "hot" weather condition (e.g., temperature between 70 and 90 degrees or temperature greater than 70 degrees).

- The data signal may be combined with other data signals, such as weather data being combined with gender data (e.g., if the weather is cold AND the user is male, show a particular men's jacket and if the user is female, show a women's coat instead).

- Certain rules need to be used to narrow down the choices before choosing specific values of data signals. For example, it might be important to narrow down the city before selecting sporting events that may be occurring in that city, so a message could be "Seattle, it's time to get out to watch the Seahawks with an ice-cold Bud...."

A "default" should always be set up as it is possible that none of the rules and conditions for a particular advertisement may be met.

Selecting rules to use for matching needs to be done with resulting matches in mind. Rules that are very narrow may result in a very small number of "hits," while very broad rules may have no significant impact due to the dynamic messaging. Combinations of rules can also rapidly narrow a selection often inadvertently. For example, testing for a specific temperature vs. a range and testing for cities rather than zip codes are common issues that may lead a high rate of "defaults," which is the creative messaging that will be delivered when there is no match.

Rules also need to support various predicates, like equal, not equal, less than, greater than, and, is not equal to, etc. They should also allow for nesting of rules; some rules can require very complex if/then/else logic that will be difficult to implement without nesting capabilities.

Rule cascading can ensure that you are able to have hits with narrow criteria while allowing for some kind of targeted messaging to still be delivered when the narrow criteria are not met. For example, while it is very compelling for an ad to message about the outcome of a baseball game, because that happens only after the game has concluded, having some broader criteria (e.g., weather) that run at a lower priority ensures that there is always a fallback and the default is delivered only as the last resort.

It may also be desirable to set weights for rules. Weights allow rules to be tested to ensure which creative messaging combinations are resulting in the highest user engagement or conversions.

The automatic prioritization of rules and relative weights of rules is often referred to as *rule optimization*, and various algorithms have been developed to alter rule priorities based on analysis of campaign results.

11

The Role of Programmatic Platforms in Personalized Advertising

It is not clear whether the push for dynamic and personalized advertising came about as a result of the major shift to programmatic media buying or whether these two simply happened at the same time. It seems like it is most likely the former, for a few possible reasons.

Programmatic media buying platforms have brought a lot of scale and efficiency to media buying. Brands have adopted programmatic platforms because of the cost and process efficiencies that these platforms have brought to the table. The traditional media buying process involves spreadsheets, slick media salespeople, ad networks with suspect inventory, and the never-ending back-and-forth on pricing. Even though I use the term *traditional* here, I don't mean that it is not being done any more. It certainly is, but I believe that this will be referred to as the traditional model in the next few years, when programmatic buying becomes pervasive and the most widely accepted way of buying media.

While the media buying process has been scaled in a big way with programmatic buying, the creative and ad production process is still being done the old way: It is highly manual and time-consuming, and it slows down the whole process of programmatic media buying. In addition to all of this, programmatic buying means the creative has to be compromised as programmatic buying today can largely be done only for basic banner sizes and other basic ad formats. So while traditional media buying allowed for "high-impact" creative, we now have to work much harder to achieve the same kind of impact in banner ads.

Using dynamic and personalized creative is a novel way to increase relevance and therefore engagement. When advertisements are personalized, even basic creative works much harder for brands when they don't have the large high-impact formats available but like the flexibility and cost-effectiveness of programmatic media buying.

Publishers are realizing that they are better off selling their inventory programmatically to the highest bidder than living with 50% to 60% fills. They have already realized that the direct sales model for standard ad inventory will not be sustainable due to the high costs of sales and the low-CPM yields via programmatic media buying platforms. They have therefore turned their efforts to providing smaller numbers of impressions of higher-impact units usually sold as sponsorships and high-CPM run-of-site packages.

This has effectively bifurcated the market into highly automated programmatic buying for scale and price efficiency and custom advertisements. For the brands that can afford it, custom high-impact executions are available as sponsorship packages on premium sites. There is almost nothing in the middle.

While the push for programmatic advertising has brought tremendous scale to media buying, it has had an unfortunate side effect of pushing the industry back to the basic small banner ads that we were close to getting rid of. This also is a throwback to the earlier mantra of reach at the lowest possible cost instead of trying to gain relevance and engagement.

Personalized advertising allows brands to be relevant while still retaining the scale that programmatic buying platforms provide. By utilizing dynamic ads which ensure that the right messaging and content are delivered to individuals, higher engagement can be gained without any significant loss in scale or increase in costs.

As they tap into personalized advertising, many brands have started to think of display advertising as more of a publishing model than a campaign model. In other words, instead of thinking in terms of successive campaign cycles, they think in terms of evergreen media on programmatic platforms within which they can deliver specific messaging to their audience, customized very specifically to audience needs.

Say that a brand has a certain budget per month for lead generation. It could launch successive campaigns, with all the work being
restarted and completed for each campaign cycle. On the other hand,
evergreen media and personalized ad technology allow brands to avoid
the significant overhead of creative updates/refreshes and instead
continue to use dynamic ad technology to swap out creative elements,
change messaging, and also optimize creative and messaging to obtain
the best results from a programmatic media buy. This model looks a
bit like the social media publishing model, where brands continuously
post stories and messages they hope their audience is listening to.

This style of campaign execution also allows brands to execute in-
the-moment messaging, as they are already in market with a campaign
and simply have to change the messaging in their advertisements
without having to go through the whole cycle of campaign planning
and launch, which may often take so much time that the moment
may have passed. With dynamic ad serving technology, these kinds of
constant changes to creative messages can be accomplished without
having to re-create the ads and redo the campaign setup. Rather, a
brand can dynamically alter just components of the ad related to the
offer while the campaign is still in flight.

A curious side effect of this kind of change to how campaigns are
launched is a change in the way media is bought. Using programmatic
buying platforms, brands can now execute annual buys that give them
the benefit of pricing and also give them the flexibility of launching
messaging and creative changes into that same media.

This goes back to the upfront media model, where brands can
buy just like they do for TV today: media that can be used through
the year for launching campaigns. Dynamic advertising technology
enables such upfront media buys to be used through the year for various campaigns, special offers, new product launches, etc., without
having to go through the whole process each time.

One of the emerging models in programmatic media buying that
could prove to bring about even greater media efficiencies using data
is triggering the media buy using external data signals. For example,
an allergy medication campaign could be set up with programmatic
bid pricing and such but be activated and run only when pollen counts
are high or when air quality is low. Other examples would be activating

a campaign for emergency supplies when a hurricane or storm warning is activated and activating a campaign for warm drinks when the temperature drops.

Programmatic media buying has had a profound impact on the advertising industry and presents tremendous price and scale efficiencies but perhaps at a cost in terms of engagement and relevance to a brand's audience. Personalized advertising can help brands retain the scale and price efficiencies while increasing relevance. It also simplifies and allows brands to spend more time on messaging and communication and less time on trying to find that magical creative concept that will wow everyone.

12 ————————————

Ad Formats

Personalized advertisements can be delivered in almost any ad format by modern ad serving platforms. However, the techniques and limitations vary a bit from format to format.

Today, advertising formats are broadly categorized into banner, video, and mobile advertising. Native advertising is an emerging format that is used widely; however, the standard and definitions for native advertising are still in infant stages.

The following sections discuss the three categories just mentioned. For examples of various personalized/dynamic ad formats, visit www.jivox.com/ad-gallery/dynamic.

Banner/Rich Media Personalization

Banner and in-banner rich media formats are the most popular ad formats for personalization. They have the advantage of being available on most sites. Also, via programmatic buying platforms, the ad standards supported are not very advanced, and so the ads can indeed be developed once and run everywhere.

One of the emerging challenges with personalization using display banner ads has become the number of people using tablets and other mobile devices. While banner advertising is often not thought of as having to do with mobile advertising, the fact of the matter is that over 30% to 40% of banner ads do end up rendering on mobile devices. The reason for this is that most publishers use a single website to deliver content to users, regardless of what device they are on. If the content is being delivered to all devices, so are the ads.

Rendering ads to mobile devices poses one rather significant problem: Most of the technology used to develop personalized ads (especially of the older DCO variety) uses ad serving platforms that build their personalization capabilities using Flash technology. And as we all know, Flash does not work on mobile devices. This means that as many as 30% to 40% of the ads do not render correctly on the devices they are delivered to.

Modern dynamic/personalized ad platforms resolve this issue by using HTML5 to render dynamic ads and also do most of the processing of rules and triggers in the back end—agnostic of the device the ads will be delivered to.

This issue is largely being resolved by the next generation of ad serving platforms, and display banners are a great way to deliver personalized advertising.

Video Personalization

Personalizing video ads is a great way to deliver targeted advertising using the ad format that is a favorite among brand advertisers because it closely resembles TV advertising.

Personalizing video ads has been made much easier due to the emergence of an IAB standard called VPAID (video player-ad interface definition), which allows video ads to be customized with all kinds of interactive features and messaging overlays. A brand can actually customize the ad experience to a specific user.

This method of personalizing video is the most scalable because it does not require multiple video assets but rather overlays customized messaging in a single video asset.

Another approach is to actually create as many versions of the video file as there are versions of the personalization. A few tools in the market enable this kind of personalization. However, when the number of creative variants gets into the hundreds or thousands— which is not uncommon—it becomes incredibly difficult to manage the process of building the assets. This process is also not truly dynamic. Take, for example, a creative idea to display the current weather in the video; this cannot be done with the multiple-versions method because it would result in 30 or 40 videos just to show all temperature values. If other variables (e.g., location) are involved, the variations could get into the hundreds or thousands very quickly. With the overlay method, you would need only one video file and can overlay that with a display of the temperature.

Creating many versions of the video also has a significant disadvantage: Even the slightest change in the creative or messaging could trigger a significant amount of work as each video file has to be reconverted and uploaded to the ad serving system. With the VPAID method, which enables overlays to be placed on a video, such changes can be very simply accomplished without even touching the video file in any manner.

Mobile Ads Personalization

Personalizing mobile advertisements is very similar to doing so in the desktop world, and it faces similar associated challenges.

Personalized mobile ads have a significant advantage over desktop display formats in that they generally have a good level of viewability, given the small form factors of mobile devices.

One of the significant hurdles, though, is the challenge with implementing cookies on mobile devices. As discussed elsewhere in this book, several mechanisms have emerged that are helping advertisers get around this issue, so this is unlikely to be a significant challenge going forward.

For mobile ad formats, due to typically lower bandwidth than in desktop environments, during the creative/production process, extra care much be exercised with the weight of individual dynamic elements and the overall weight of the ad itself.

13

Planning for a Data-Driven Dynamic Advertising Campaign

Planning for a personalized advertising campaign can be daunting, given the number of possible data signals, creative variations, etc. However, putting a process in place for how the campaign will come together can save everyone a lot of time and effort.

One of the key challenges with personalized ad campaigns is the creative approvals needed. Managing this process well can make the difference between a process that seems to take forever and one that comes together quickly and launches on time.

Some of the key steps in a successful launch of a personalized ad campaign are described in this chapter.

Identify Key Data Signals

The brand team needs to explore the available data signals and identify what is relevant to the brand. This involves trying to identify possible correlations between consumers of the brand and the data signals. The question to ask would be "Does the data signal's value, or its presence or absence, influence the engagement with or purchase of the brand?" Let's look at some examples.

The following table of brands and signals shows clearly which data signals might be relevant:

	Weather	Profile	Sports	Entertainment	Geography	Social
Audi	✓	✓	✓	✓		✓
Lipitor		✓	✓	✓	✓	
L'Oreal	✓	✓		✓	✓	✓
Wells Fargo		✓			✓	✓
Starbucks	✓					✓

This table is meant to be a guide rather than a list of hard-and-fast rules for these brands. Whether the brands and signals align depends, of course, on the specific product being advertised and the overall strategy for the campaign.

Identify Specific Variables and Granularity of Signals

After identifying key data signals, the next step is to identify how granular the data signal should be. For example, in terms of weather as a signal, is the brand sensitive to temperature, precipitation (e.g., whether it is snowing), or just overall weather conditions?

Similarly, for sporting events, the brand may have more affinity to specific sporting events than to others. For example, luxury brands have a higher affinity to sports like golf and tennis, while more mainstream brands may look at sports like football and baseball since those games are enjoyed by most people. There may also be gender differences to factor in. For example, L'Oreal may choose women's sports rather than men's sports.

Identify Trigger Conditions

The next step is to figure out what specific conditions of the data signals should trigger delivery of a specific creative or messaging. This is ideally done after the two steps just described. It could be done by creating an all-inclusive list of data signals and their associated variables, in a spreadsheet that looks something like this:

Data Signal(s)	Trigger Condition	Message	Images
Weather, City	Weather=Rainy & City=Seattle	Hey, Seattle, it's been pouring. Time to hit the gym.	Animated gym scene, treadmill, Nike jogging shoe
Weather, City	Weather=Cold & City=Seattle	Hey, Seattle, it's freezing. Warm up with a workout.	Animated image of huddled person and person on treadmill, Nike jogging shoe
Weather, City	Weather=Hot & City=Seattle	Hey, Seattle, it's our annual Sunny day.	Golf range, golfer in Nike golf shoes
Weather, City	Weather=Warm & City=Seattle	Hey, Seattle, pull off the covers: It's Sunny.	Animated sunrise and tennis game, Nike tennis shoe
Weather, City	Default	Hey there, is today that day?	Golf range, golfer in Nike golf shoes

A creative agency typically creates such spreadsheets. It may develop assets for each of the trigger conditions after it has built this spreadsheet. This is an important step as it can get quite chaotic and confusing if the whole picture of what triggers to use and assets to build is not defined up front.

It is also important to develop creative messaging for a default condition that does not meet any of the rules. For example, in the preceding example, you'd need messaging to use if the ad is viewed outside Seattle or if none of the weather conditions are met.

Crafting trigger conditions also requires some thought because it is possible to end up with very few impressions delivering personalized creative if the trigger conditions are narrow. For example, in the above rules, you might also want to specify suburbs of Seattle or perhaps use the zip code or DMA instead of a specific city name. This is a bit of a trade-off because folks in Bellevue may not like seeing an ad that assumes they are in Seattle. Luckily, from a production standpoint, messaging in an ad is easy to render because you can simply use the city name from the geographic lookup and render it in the ad instead of having to build hundreds of text images.

This trigger analysis can get a little tricky. My company recently worked on a campaign that had an image associated with several zip codes. The zip database and the associated zip codes provided had only 2,500 entries compared to the 43,191 zip codes in the United States, so basic math said that a lot of default ads would be served. Therefore, we ended up working out a proximity calculation, which gave us much wider coverage to ensure a low rate of defaults.

It is not always possible to accurately calculate the likely number of defaults in a campaign because it sometimes depends on the distribution of media and demographics. In other words, if the media is skewed in an opposite direction from the audiences the ads are being personalized for, a higher default rate can be expected.

There are a couple techniques for mitigating this problem:

- Match up broader targeting with the personalization. For example, if a women's cosmetic product ad is being personalized in several different ways and a default is assumed when it is served to men, of course statistically at least 50% of the ads will be defaults. In this case, targeting the ad or media buy to a female demographic would greatly reduce the default rate.

- Have a data signal and trigger conditions that will always be true (e.g., weather). If an ad campaign is personalized to refer to local sporting events, what should the ad say on days when there is no local sporting event? Every day has weather, so that would be a data signal to incorporate into the personalization instead of serving up a default ad.

Serving up default creative is not altogether bad. It can often serve to benchmark the personalization against a nonpersonalized default creative to get a sense of brand lift from serving the personalized ad.

Ideate and Define Creative Canvas and Variable Elements

At this point, the creative team comes in and starts to think of the creative canvas on which to deliver personalized creative and messaging. Usually this involves defining what parts of the ad will remain constant and what parts of the ad will be personalized to the user. In the simplest case, the only thing changing in the ad may be some copy. However, the creative team should consider defining other elements in the ad to be variable, such as a skin that reflects weather, an animation showing the team colors for the sporting event, or maybe skins or animations showing the geography being delivered to.

This is a fine balance because the more variable creative elements are, the bigger the matrix will get, and the longer the approvals will take. However, the other extreme is an ad that is simply not interesting enough to get attention; in fact, consumers may not even be aware that the ad is dynamic and personalized to them.

One of the decisions that has to be made at this stage is whether approval of the basic canvas and all the assets for the variations are sufficient for approvals or whether the brand team wants to approve all the finished ads. The latter approach can get challenging if the number of variants gets large. For example, a campaign that has messaging for all the sporting events over a six-month period could have several hundred approvals, especially if combined with another data signal like weather.

Another decision to be made is what the default ad would be. The default is the version of the ad that would be served if none of the programmed conditions were being met in the dynamic ad.

Produce Creative

Creative production is the process of building out all the variations of the ads and messaging. If the above steps have been diligently followed, this process is likely to go much more smoothly since the data signals, trigger conditions, and creative messaging for each would all have been decided on and approved.

Production can be very challenging if it's done using a technology platform that is not designed for dynamic ads. The key here is that with creative production and ad serving platforms that are not designed for dynamic ads, each creative variant will have to be built as a separate ad. This could create significant issues and delays in production since each ad has to be separately developed and put through a QA process.

Changes to creative concepts or assets can also cause significant ripple effects on ad production if individual ads are built for each creative variation.

The solution to this issue is to first identify components of an ad that will remain the same in each variant of the ad—for example, the skin, logo, perhaps some animation, etc. This should be separated out from the variable components of the ad, such as messages, videos, map locations, etc. This needs to be a key consideration during the creative design process to avoid major delays.

Newer technology platforms (see Chapter 18, "Technology for Developing Data-Driven Advertisements") are capable of delivering hundreds or thousands of creative variations in a single ad as they have a dynamic content management system that can house all the creative assets and serve them based on data signals and trigger conditions.

The second important feature needed in a dynamic advertising platform is the data feeds and rule execution engine. In older-generation ad platforms, the rules have to be hand coded, making the whole process very error prone and time-consuming. So it is important to ask technology vendors how trigger conditions are specified in the platform: Are they specified via a UI or hand coded, and how easy are they to change?

The reason this is critical is that when it comes time to optimize the campaign, optimizing hand-coded rules and trigger conditions can be very messy or even impossible.

Identify Key Metrics to Be Measured

At this stage, it is usually a good idea to identify the metrics that will be measured in order to determine the success of the campaign and also to optimize creative. This often requires that some kind of configuration and setup be done. In modern dynamic ad platforms, the measurement process is much more dynamic, and all variable components of an ad are automatically recognized and recorded. Older ad platforms often require extensive tagging work in the ad code, and so it is very critical to have all that done and tested extensively before campaign launch.

Key metrics for performance-oriented dynamic ad campaigns are usually click-throughs, view-throughs, and conversions. On the other hand, branding campaigns tend to focus on other metrics, like engagement time, interactions, and video views.

Unless personalized ads are highly interactive, they are often best measured using brand lift studies. Often users see an ad with relevant messaging, and it causes the brand to register, but the users may not click on or otherwise interact with the ad. A brand lift study can usually get a measurement of impact on the brand in terms of recall.

Measuring viewability may also be key for personalized ad campaigns because they rely significantly on users seeing the ad and being drawn to it due to the personalized nature of the messaging. If an ad campaign has a low number of viewable impressions, the impact of the personalization will simply not be seen because there is not enough exposure of the creative to users to create sufficient lift in engagement.

I have seen significant differences in engagement metrics between the same personalized ad run on a direct publisher with higher viewability compared to an ad network buy with much lower viewability of the ads.

Identify Optimization Criteria

Most personalized/dynamic ad campaigns can benefit significantly from optimization. For campaigns that are more branding oriented, there may be multiple creative concepts or data signals being used to vary creative messaging, and so it would be useful to know which ones are the most effective. For example, if a campaign has weather-based creative and creative tied to local sporting events, it may not be clear which one is performing better, and being able to look at various metrics related to both data signals/rules will allow for optimization to produce better engagement.

Modern dynamic ad platforms can automatically optimize performance based on the selection of a metric to optimize with. For example, the optimization could be around interaction rates or conversions, depending on whether it is a branding or performance campaign.

If automated optimization is being used, it is important to ensure that the platform is capable of continuous sampling to ensure that changes in engagement levels for certain data signals are factored in immediately. For example, if a weather-triggered creative is being lowered in priority because sporting events are doing better, it might be that when the actual weather turns more extreme, users may respond better to a weather creative. In other words, normal routine weather may not trigger much of a user response, so it is important for the system to continuously monitor the weather creative via sampling to ensure that any spikes in engagement will quickly cause it to be rotated back in at a higher priority.

To develop a better understanding of what methods may be available for optimization, see the section "Optimization of Personalized Ads" in Chapter 14, "Measurement, ROI, and Optimization of Personalized Ad Campaigns."

Define Dynamic Data Signals

Certain dynamic data signals cannot be determined or programmed up front as there needs to be human involvement to interpret and come up with messaging or creative elements for the data signal. This process needs to be defined up front so the brand can take advantage of it. For example, a brand that wants to look at top Twitter trending topics and figure out what messaging to publish will need to set up a process to do so.

This is time-sensitive information; that is, if it takes more than a few weeks to publish the trend, it may no longer be a trend by the time it gets published and therefore may no longer be relevant or interesting.

Brands that want to leverage these kinds of dynamic data signals should consider a newsroom-like process and team, where the team can quickly assess the news or event and then decide on messaging for it, create any needed assets, and push out the updates to the ad via the dynamic ad platform.

In addition to being used with consumer interest–related events like sports and entertainment, this kind of model can also be used to handle competitive pricing changes, product announcements, etc., where time is of the essence in being able to get a message out.

Preview the Ad and Get Creative Approvals

The subject of previews and creative approvals is one that often comes up during discussions to deliver personalized/dynamic advertisements. In general, the system being used to produce and deliver ads must be capable of showing in preview mode all the possible creative variations as well as filter by certain triggers, rules, and creative sizes/types to allow for narrowing into a specific set of creative for approval.

The question of whether someone will approve each and every permutation of a creative is really one that the brand/creative and media teams need to evaluate and explore, both in terms of necessity and feasibility. With campaigns that may have several thousand creative variations, it might be a process of sampling what works best rather than one of approving every single creative combination.

In certain verticals, it is imperative that the brand be able to review and approve every single creative variant prior to launch. The financial services industry and the pharmaceuticals industry are two examples where brands often require that each creative variant be approved before launch. Depending on how stringent the process is, sometimes this can be done just at the asset/mock level, but often approvers require actual versions of the live ads in previews before they will approve the ads for launch.

Handle Final QA and Launch

Dynamic and personalized advertisements require a somewhat different approach to QA than traditional static ads. The QA process has to replicate the dynamic data signals, rules, and ad serving in a test environment in order to ensure that the correct creative variants are being rendered for each data signal and rule combination. Here again, modern dynamic ad platforms have extensive capabilities to use preview tags and pages to conduct extensive testing to ensure that all the signals, rules, ads, and reporting are working correctly and as expected. These platforms also have extensive facilities to test rules and signals to troubleshoot and discover issues well ahead of campaign launch.

14

Measurement, ROI, and Optimization of Personalized Ad Campaigns

Reporting and measurement of personalized ad campaigns are critical to marketers. In the earlier days of dynamic creative optimization (DCO), when ads were not quite personalized, a lot of performance data that was collected was often used to determine which creative performed the best.

With personalized ads, the creative variants of an ad can quickly get into the hundreds and thousands, and so collecting very fine-grained data about each creative variant that was delivered and on what site and placement it was delivered becomes very critical.

Often various programmatic media strategies are employed in a campaign (e.g., retargeting), and in such cases it is important to record that data to understand which strategies are yielding the best results.

Measurement of ROI for dynamic and personalized advertising campaigns can vary based on the goals of the campaign. In general, dynamic ad campaigns can be separated broadly into performance (or direct-response) marketing efforts and branding efforts. Most campaigns have some level of a mix of both of these; they are usually set up and measured to optimize either leads and conversions or brand engagement.

Performance, or direct-response, campaigns that employ dynamic or personalized content often try to determine what types of content or creative are producing the best results. Measures here often include the following key metrics:

- **Click-through rates:** Measures how often users clicked through the ad to a web page

- **View-through rates:** Measures how often users saw the ad and then reached the advertiser's website via other means (e.g., search)

- **Conversion rates:** Measures how often users, after having seen the ad or clicked through the ad, actually purchased a product

It is critical, therefore, that performance-oriented dynamic ad campaigns not only measure these metrics but also report on them, broken down by the creative variants, so it becomes easier to optimize a campaign for better performance.

For campaigns that are much more focused on brand awareness, personalized advertising can be very impactful in creating awareness and engagement. However, as with many other branding campaigns, it may also be more challenging to measure the impact of personalized advertising. Brand lift studies, which have long been used to determine the lift caused by branding campaigns, are still a very effective means to measure the impact of personalized advertising.

It is often beneficial also to run an A/B test of standard creative versus personalized creative, although the one note of caution in comparing results is that the comparisons have to be made on "like media." For example, comparing personalized ads running on a programmatic platform with basic ads running on direct bought media may show results that are misleading because programmatic ad delivery is often associated with lower-quality inventory, poor viewability of ads, and sometimes fraud, all of which can impact metrics in measure lift.

It is pretty obvious but needs to be stated that much like a good creative, a personalized creative has to first be seen by users for them to engage, so viewability of ads must be relatively high in order to be able to measure any significant lift in engagement due to serving up personalized creative.

It is also important to point out that obsessing too much on directly measurable immediate outcomes of personalized ads can lead to the conclusion that the ROI is not there when in fact it may be that it cannot be easily measured. This is similar to personalized service being used to build loyalty. When you walk into a hotel, if the hotel staff remember you and your preferences from your previous trip because their system kept track, are you not more likely to be loyal to the hotel? It is pretty clear intuitively that personalization makes customers feel that the brand is smart and is putting in the extra effort to make them comfortable and show them that it does care about their preferences and choices. Personalized advertising is simply an extension to the personalized services, apps, websites, and numerous ways each day that we appreciate the idea that a brand cares about what we like and don't like and will do what it takes to respect our time and the inevitable interruption an advertisement takes out of a person's life.

The other way to look at ROI of personalized advertising is by looking at media spend. It's a bit of what the legendary businessman and marketing genius John Wanamaker said: "Half the money I spend on advertising is wasted; the trouble is I don't know which half." The most compelling argument that personalized advertising does produce great ROI, even it is not exactly measurable, has to do with media wastage, with messages that are simply irrelevant to the audience the advertisement is being served to.

Let's look at an example of a razor brand. While each brand offers many shapes and sizes of razors, they are primarily split into razors for men and razors for women. Running an untargeted advertisement of razors for men means that 50% of the media spend on that ad is wasted right off the bat. Also, it is likely that a woman seeing an ad for a male razor will find it annoying and completely irrelevant. Now let's take this a step further. Say that the razor model being advertised is the lowest-priced throwaway variety; with this ad, men who will simply never use such razors will also find the ad annoying and irrelevant; say that this is another 50% of the males who see the ad. Now say that of the remaining 25% of viewers who are indeed the relevant audience for the razor, perhaps 75% are football fans and will respond well to messaging that references the upcoming 49ers game, and the rest are baseball fans who will find a football reference in the ad completely annoying and irrelevant. I could go on and on with this, but you get the idea. From a media-buying ROI perspective, if the razor campaign were run without any of the personalizations possible, as much as 80% of the media may simply be wasted and have little or no impact on prospective buyers of the razor.

The media industry's solution to this issue has been to target ads to audiences. However, targeting does not take advantage of the micro-segments of data that the brand actually often has data about. In addition, the buying and execution of so many micro-segments of media is impossible, and the costs and complexity may wipe out any benefit from doing so. It is a well-known fact that the more targeted a media buy is, the more expensive it gets. Imagine buying lots of micro-targeted segments at high CPMs just to try to reach specific micro-audiences. Sounds like a money- and sanity-losing proposition. Furthermore, most targeted media buys—even from programmatic platforms using demand-side platforms (DSPs)—only provide targeting with third-party data, and this simply does not utilize the wealth of first-party data that a brand has gathered about its customers that it is not using.

Much of the data that can be used to deliver personalized advertising to individuals actually exists in many cases with the brand and is not made available to an advertising campaign. For example, past purchase activity, categories of products purchased, browsing activity on a brand's website, and customer service records all provide very valuable information that will help personalize advertising. However, when ad campaigns are run with just basic audience targeting, which is largely all that is available today from direct or programmatic media, none of this data is being put to any good use for the brand.

Personalized advertising essentially takes a presumed broad and general audience for a product and ensures that each micro-segment of preferences has targeted and relevant messaging delivered to it. It also ensures that such campaigns can be executed at scale.

Personalized advertising also does not rely solely on media capabilities to deliver relevance and ROI on advertising but rather uses vast amounts of data to intelligently message and engage with a brand's audience.

Ultimately, personalized advertising will have a positive and measurable impact on product sales and so has to be sustained for long enough to see that impact through. As with any other marketing program, the ultimate determinant of success is sales. It is a question of when and how the impact is seen.

Managing Costs for Personalization

One of the topics that comes up in discussions about ROI is, of course, the costs of the technology, people, and process that need to be factored in to make sure there is positive ROI to the efforts and activities described in this book.

I look at investments in three categories:

- One-time data and content infrastructure investments
- Per-campaign costs
- Ongoing data infrastructure maintenance costs

Data infrastructure investments can be very basic in nature and may range from the placement of tracking tags on a brand's website (which usually doesn't cost anything) all the way to building very robust data management infrastructure (like the razor example described previously, which could run into several hundred thousand dollars to possibly millions of dollars for large brands). An incremental mode of investment may be best in order to harvest ROI along the path to having a complete and robust data management environment that can be used in all manner of personalized campaigns.

Data management infrastructure should also be looked upon as a capital investment that will pay off over many years, and so from an IT investment and accounting standpoint, it can often be amortized over several years so that it doesn't impact marketing budgets immediately and take away from critical day-to-day marketing budgets and programs.

It may also be best to use outside consulting firms or resources from ad platform vendors as many of these projects require heavy upfront investment of resources and specific expertise that may not be available in-house and may not be required except for maintenance on a go-forward basis.

This infrastructure should also be viewed as foundational for all marketing activities—not just display advertising but email marketing, social media marketing, etc.—and so the costs can be amortized across those programs, too.

Ongoing data infrastructure costs in general are much smaller than the initial setup costs. Content infrastructure again can vary quite a bit, depending on the quantity and quality of content to be produced. If the content will be produced only for specific campaigns, the personnel and other capital expenditure costs may not be worth it, especially to have a team on call for the few campaigns that need it.

Some brands that view content marketing as strategic and feel that they should constantly produce content have set up internal content production teams that continuously produce content for the various marketing activities they engage in continuously. A fully functioning content team requires creative strategists, content designers, and developers, as well as possibly studio equipment for video, editing software, production software, computers, etc. Again, a lot of this investment is infrastructure, and some of it can be capital investments that will pay off and amortize over time.

Per-campaign costs include media costs, which are often the largest piece, and then content production costs and ad serving costs. Media costs for personalized advertising are the same as media costs for standard advertising with no personalization since all the personalization is done using ad serving software.

Ad production and campaign setup costs on a per-campaign basis are usually less than 5% of media costs. Ad serving fees can range from 5% to 10% of media costs and sometimes will include the ad production and campaign setup costs, especially for large campaigns or larger commitments to the ad serving platform vendor. If third-party data is being purchased for use in the campaign, that could add about 5% of media costs to the campaign, depending on the type of data being used and the vendors used for the data. Ad serving platforms sometimes have bundled prices that include some of the data as part of the ad serving fees; the pricing for data purchased this way is usually less than the cost of a la carte purchases of data.

Brands are increasingly looking at some of these costs as really being costs of selling rather than looking at marketing as a cost center. So marketing activities such as personalized advertising, which create better brand engagement, conversions, and sales should ideally be viewed in terms of lifts in sales and so should be weighed against the impact on sales. The challenge, of course, in many cases is being able to measure and attribute a lift in sales to personalized advertising. While online conversions can be accurately measured, offline conversion (e.g., a user seeing an advertisement and then going to a retail store and buying it) is hard to measure.

Marketers spend millions of dollars on TV advertising and have no tangible way of tying it back to sales, and yet they do spend the money because they know that it does impact sales positively, even if it is not directly and empirically measurable. Similarly, personalized advertising needs to be weighed in terms of the benefit of engagement and brand building, even when it cannot be tied directly to online purchases. User purchase behavior is no longer a linear process, and there are many influences that eventually trigger purchases.

Optimization of Personalized Ads

Optimization of personalized ads is often used as an additional way to increase engagement. The basic premise of personalized ads is that you predetermine and preoptimize outcomes by selecting user preferences up front and delivering to them the precisely tailored messaging matching their preferences. In addition, there may still be some benefit to applying optimization techniques, especially when the input data signals themselves may not be very precise or may not even be specific to a user preference but may instead be environmental in nature.

Basic forms of optimization focus on the primary goal of the campaign and flag the creative variant that performs best for that goal. For example, if the goal is to produce high click-through rates, the personalization system would automatically select that creative variant.

As described in the following sections, several methods are used to select the best-performing combination of creative and content, depending on the kinds of data signals, complexity of rules, and amounts and types of data available for optimization.

A/B Testing

A/B testing is the simplest form of testing to determine what creative or content combination is producing the best results. A/B testing involves creating two variants of messaging or creative and running them in parallel in a single campaign, with an equal exposure of both variants to the users who see the ad. The campaign is then optimized to serve the version that is producing the best performance between the two.

Basic versions of A/B tests used in optimization often don't produce the best results because they don't factor in user fatigue to messaging and they don't conclusively determine one variant to be better than the other. More sophisticated A/B testing–based optimization algorithms often perform sampling with both creative variants to ensure that any changes in the performance of either creative is constantly monitored and factored into the weighting of the creative.

It may also be that a creative variant that wasn't performing too well at a point in time may start performing well. For example, certain messaging may work better on a weekend than on a weekday. Therefore, the ability to constantly test and evaluate combinations of creative is vital to campaign performance.

Multivariate Testing

Multivariate testing is essentially an extension of A/B testing that is used to determine which of many variable messaging and creative elements in an ad may be producing the best results.

For example, an ad may have a set of different images or animations, combined with different calls to action, such as "special offer," "reduced rate," "learn more," etc. The idea with multivariate testing is to figure out which combination of images, animations, and calls to action result in the highest engagement by users.

While it is an expansion on the idea of A/B testing, multivariate testing does introduce a rather complex set of metrics and permutations and combinations that need to be analyzed in order to determine what truly is engaging users better.

Multivariate testing is best combined with multivariate optimization, where instead of trying to analyze very large amounts of data to understand which combinations are leading to the best performance outcomes, algorithms in an ad serving platform can be used to automatically select the combination that produces the best results.

Software built into dynamic ad serving platforms can of course analyze hundreds—or even thousands—of such variables and can select the best combinations of creative and messaging in an ad. In order to do so, the software needs to know what to optimize for. For example, performance-oriented campaigns often want to optimize for click-through rates, while branding campaigns may have a wider range for performance metrics, such as interaction rates, video views, gallery views, etc. Once you select a metric (or metrics), the software can then analyze the data to determine the best combination of creative and messaging to achieve best results for the selected metric(s).

In order for A/B or multivariate testing to be effective, in general, with more variables, the larger the sample set needs to be. This is a bit of an exponential sizing issue. For example, a campaign with 4 variables needs to be not twice as large as a campaign with only 2 variables but actually 12 times as large in order to be effective. This is often referred to as the *factorial problem*, where as more variables are added, the permutations and combinations can become daunting, and incorrect conclusions may be drawn if the sample set it too small.

This issue can be further exacerbated if new variables are introduced into the campaign while in flight, as the new variables may not have been exposed to users as much as existing ones, and so any comparison of data between them is likely to be faulty.

Artificial Intelligence/Predictive Algorithms and Machine Learning

There is a lot of room for improvement in how personalized and dynamic ad campaigns are optimized. Most dynamic ad campaigns have had only a handful of variables (in fact, usually one or two), so optimization—whether done by humans or algorithmically—has been pretty straightforward.

As Big Data plays a more important role in personalization of advertisements, the number of data signals, the complexity of rules, and the sheer number of outcomes can increase exponentially. As that happens, human optimization simply cannot be done except perhaps after the fact, forensically, when there is little to no opportunity to impact the outcome. Algorithmic optimization will have to be done, but even there, simple linear regression algorithms that can handle linear relationships and correlations may not be able to sufficiently create improved outcomes, given the vast number of data inputs and resulting measurements that have to be processed to predict performance.

With so many variables, you need very sophisticated algorithms that utilize machine learning, artificial intelligence, and other non-linear algorithms that can make predictions about outcomes based on learning from large data sets of input. In the world of computer science, this is often referred to as *machine learning*—the idea being that when many variables with very complex relationships between them are involved in determining outcomes, it is better and easier to learn from the data to figure out the formula than to try to figure out a formula to begin with, given that the relationships between the variables may be too complex to determine an algorithm for them. This is essentially a much more advanced method of determining formulas than the "curve-fitting" methods presented in high school algebra.

There are several techniques for machine learning. All of them are well beyond the scope of this book, but I list a few of them here, with possible applications to the world of personalized advertising, so you can research them on your own:

- **Bayesian networks:** A Bayesian network is a way of representing related variables in the form of a directed graph. Probabilities can be assigned to each node in the graph, and it is possible to predict outcomes by examining data and "learning" from data points.

- **Decision trees:** A decision tree is a useful visual representation of how decisions influence outcomes and can be used to evaluate data and rules to determine the path to take when it comes to rendering the right creative that will likely produce the best performance.

- **Association rule learning:** This is a machine learning algorithm that is suited to working with very large data sets where the relationships between variables are not clear and have to be determined. For example, a retailer may be able to make the correlation that whenever an advertisement has an image of a person smiling along with a prompt with a special offer, users tend to engage more; or perhaps images of a family tend to drive higher engagement for certain types of products.

When it comes to optimization, it is often best to walk before you run as optimization can become extraordinarily complex without any measurable positive impact. Sometimes the most intuitively obvious rules and optimizations may have a much bigger impact than any algorithm can. Human emotions, which are at the heart of purchase and engagement behavior, are very hard to mimic in algorithms, and so in some sense, humans armed with both algorithms and technology may indeed have the best outcomes.

When starting out with personalized advertising, it may be best not to focus too much on optimization because, after all, unlike with the earlier discipline of DCO, which relies on algorithms to produce better results, the hope with personalized advertising is that by using data as an input, we might produce the best matches anyway between user preferences and marketing messaging, and the need to optimize beyond that may not be very fruitful.

With a data-driven approach to personalization, it is possible and often more sensible to apply these machine learning techniques to data and use those outcomes to feed the personalization of ads. For example, by analyzing raw sales data, correlations can be made as to what kinds of products are purchased by certain individuals, and this data in turn can be used to personalize ads for those individuals.

15

Data-Driven Dynamic
Ad Products for Publishers

Most of the discussion in this book has been about marketers personalizing advertising and using data they have collected or have access to. In many cases, though, marketers who do not have the knowledge or infrastructure to launch personalized ad campaigns may still want to try it out or even potentially just have someone else figure it out for them. In these cases, dynamic advertising platform providers and publishers can help brands get started while they invest in their own internal capabilities.

Certain large publishers have been offering such data-driven dynamic ads. For example, Yahoo has offered "Smart Ads" for some time now, using Yahoo Weather, Yahoo Finance, and other data. eBay and Amazon, in a limited fashion, are offering ads personalized with their product listing data. The Weather Channel also offers some weather- and profile-enabled ad products. In 2015 and beyond, I expect that most large publishers will start offering data-enabled ad products.

Publishers, especially large ones, have massive amounts of data about visitors to their sites. The types of data include interests (e.g., people who like sports cars vs. SUVs), the types of sports they may be interested in, their shopping habits, what they are searching for, etc. For some premium publishers, this data is somewhat permanent (i.e., not cookie based) and is available across devices. This is because these publishers have logins that serve to precisely identify users and, therefore, all the data about them can be saved using the login as a key.

The types of data-enabled ad products that publishers can offer depend to some extent on the size and scale of their audience/traffic. Very large publishers, like Yahoo, Facebook, Google, Microsoft, and AOL, can offer ad products enabled with profile data because they have the size of audience to do so, and a particular media buy can be further personalized based on subsegments of the audience on the site. For smaller publishers, this is not feasible because the media buy may be only a few million impressions, and further personalizing that may not make much sense.

Other data signals that publishers can use if they don't have large (or reliable, login-based) user profiles include the following:

- **Contextual data signals:** A food site could offer up user segments based on the food interests of the user, such as bakery, soups, entrees, desserts, etc. An automobile site may offer as context sports cars, luxury cars, SUVs, etc. It may also offer context on whether the user is interested in racing events, outdoor sports like skiing, camping, etc. This kind of signal is simply obtained by tagging various articles on the page with keywords and a taxonomy that the ads can then use to personalize the ad experience.

- **Search data signals:** Many sites have search bars in them where users can search for content within the site. A search can be a valuable indicator of user intent. For example, a search for "used Volvo review" would indicate that the user is in the market for used cars and perhaps looking specifically at Volvo cars. Similarly, a search for "nasal allergy" could be a signal for allergy products.

- **Site content–powered ads:** Several publishers have very valuable content that could enhance user engagement with a brand. For example, an outdoor sports site could offer content feeds of various outdoor sports that could be rendered in the ad and matched up with the personalization of the ad. For example, a sporting goods manufacturer could create several personalized versions of ads with various sporting goods to match the sporting activity (e.g., camping gear for camping enthusiasts, tennis gear for tennis players, etc.). Depending on what content page the ad is being served on, site content could be pulled in to match the context, and that same contextual tag would be used to inform the ad about the personalization so that the content and the ad copy/content could match.

Imagine an ad for camping gear that has the products from an outdoor brand like Patagonia. That same ad could have a feed of content related to camping from the sports enthusiast site. The content feed and the products displayed in the ad could change based on the page and context in which the ad is served.

Publisher Data Integration

One of the challenges with data-enabled personalized ad offerings from a site is that they typically have to be site served due to the fact that the ad needs to be integrated into the site's data and content. There are, however, ways to get around this by enabling a site to integrate easily with third-party ad serving platforms and to pass both site data and site content into the ad.

Site data is best passed via tag variables. A *tag variable* is a variable contained within an ad tag whose value is set at the time the ad is served on the site. Once an ad is served on the page, the page passes the value of the tag variable to the ad, and then the ad can render the correct version of the ad, based on the context of the page.

Page content can also be integrated quite easily into advertising content. Most publishers use a CMS system for their site content, and many CMS systems can provide RSS or JSON feed access to the content in the CMS system. Dynamic ad platforms often have the ability to ingest these feeds and render them into ads. This integration is usually very straightforward and does not require any custom development/programming.

The feed-based mode of integrating site content into an ad is a good way to go because the ad content will then dynamically change as the site content changes. This method of site content integration also creates a kind of "native" look and feel to the ad, resulting in much higher engagement levels for the ad. An example of such site content integration could be that an ad for Pillsbury cookie mix could integrate site content from Martha Stewart Living's site with recipes for various cookies that can be made with that cookie mix.

This kind of dynamic site content integration is typically used in native ad formats, but there is no reason it can't also be used in standard display ad formats, and it is indeed being done today by many publishers.

As media buying transitions rapidly into programmatic buying, a sizable amount of publisher ad inventory is being sold via programmatic supply-side platforms. This, in turn, is making publishers focus their direct sales efforts on more "one-of-a-kind" ad formats that can deliver high CPMs/revenue and are significantly differentiated from the kinds of ads that brands can purchase programmatically.

Personalized/dynamic ad formats are a great way for publishers to differentiate their ad products and command high premiums for that. They also create unique inventory that is not available via programmatic buys since they are integrated into site data and/or content, and that type of ad format will not be available via programmatic buying.

Many publishers are realizing that their data is also an asset that can be monetized. Clearly, creating their own ad products personalized with their own data makes a lot of sense, but in addition, publishers can package their site data and make it available to brands for targeting and personalization. Many sites already do this through basic integration with DMPs, and a few have established their own private DMPs, but this is something we are likely to see more and more, especially from the larger publishers that have massive amounts of data that is not being monetized or even used in any meaningful way.

In order to do this, though, publishers have to invest a bit more in enriching their data. Cookie data that simply states that a visitor appeared on their site may not be very valuable. On the other hand, the user's consumption of content on the site, site searches, and likes and shares of site content on social media are all very valuable data signals that can be used to personalize advertising on the site or elsewhere.

One could argue that publishers, especially large ones, should invest in building a personalization data store (PDS) similar to the one described earlier for brands to build in-house. This kind of hub of data can be a proprietary gold mine of data that the publisher can offer via ad products or directly as data products.

E-commerce Companies Become Media Companies

An interesting, rarely noticed trend in the past few years has been that companies that were primarily known for their e-commerce or e-tail offerings have quietly become sizable media companies. Amazon, eBay, and Walmart.com come to mind. Most large online retailers, of course, do display advertising on their sites, usually filled in by ad networks or DSPs.

What these three behemoths and others are starting to offer are various targeting capabilities to brands as they have a very significant wealth of data about search, browsing, and purchase behavior on their sites. It stands to reason that these online retailers will start offering much more personalized ad products to brands. Given the volume and scale of traffic they have on their sites and the wealth of data they can tap into, they could rival some of the large publishers, like Yahoo, Google, and Microsoft—both in terms of scale and reach and also in terms of the variety and scale of data assets they have.

One of the most sought-after pieces of data among marketers these days also happens to be something these publishers have: a unified identity across all devices. Many brands are facing immense challenges tracking conversions and performing attribution analysis across devices due to the lack of a single identity of a user across devices. Online retailers, unlike most web publishers, have this identity because users have to log into their sites in order to purchase products from the site. This data rivals what Facebook, Google, and Yahoo have as it's tied to the identities of particular consumers, thanks to the login information tying users across devices.

Device Companies Become Media Companies

What we thought of as digital media companies were usually either the online properties of TV and print media companies or pure digital properties like Mashable, Huffington Post, Yahoo, etc. A new kind of media company is emerging from the world of devices. We all, of course, immediately think of Apple. Apple has had a fledgling advertising business called iAd, which it offers, mostly for delivering bespoke ad products to many brands. It was once rumored that Apple was asking for $10 million minimum to run an advertising campaign using iAd, but it appears that number has since come down significantly.

The new entrants into this market are, of course, Amazon, with all its Kindle tablet and reader products, and its media business, Amazon Prime. It is not clear whether Amazon, which is definitely selling advertising products on its e-commerce site, will also seek to monetize some of its Prime content via advertising.

Samsung was until recently mostly thought of as a device company, but it is starting to introduce some media applications and has a fledgling advertising business on its connected TV products.

All the companies in this category also have a tremendous wealth of user data that could put them at a significant advantage over many media companies due to their scale and the wealth of data they have access to, thanks to the ubiquity of their devices.

It remains to be seen how aggressively these companies will pursue digital advertising models to monetize their content, but it is clear that if they did, they could become pretty significant players in the world of personalized digital advertising.

16

Developing Big Data
for Personalization

Big Data is a big buzzword with marketers these days, so it perhaps makes sense to define what we mean by *Big Data* in the context of personalized advertising.

Big Data refers to the vast amounts of data being generated outside traditional sources that, when harnessed properly, can provide a wealth of insights that can be used to customize and personalize digital advertising. The two new sources of Big Data are data gathered from mobile phones, tablets, and other wearable devices and data generated from social media. A decade ago, neither of these sources of data existed. What's unique about this data compared to all the other data that marketers have had for years is that this new data is highly personal and pertains to the likes, habits, dislikes, immediate environment, and even emotions of individuals. Another thing that is unique about this very accurate data is that it is generated and captured in real time.

For the purposes of this discussion, I use the term *Big Data* to also include traditional sources of data, such as CRM data and website activity data, which also provide valuable customer insights for marketers.

Data Sources

Data that can be used for personalization that originates from within a brand's sources is often referred to as first-party data. Today, first-party data is used to a very limited extent primarily for performance marketing campaigns and for retargeting of website visitors.

Several sources of first-party data exist within most brands. Data is often collected at most customer touch points, including retail points of sales, the brand's website, customer service, warranty service and repairs, customer financing, loyalty programs, etc.

In most organizations, unfortunately, at each of these touch points, while data is collected, it is often stored in a data silo and not available or accessible to other parts of the organization (e.g., marketing to use to make marketing more effective).

In addition to data being in various silos, the data also often uses nomenclature and is organized in such a way that it is not in a form that can be used for marketing without extensive rework.

Many organizations have invested in building data warehouses and data marts internally (often using software from my first company, Informatica). These data warehouses contain aggregated data organized in a way that makes it easy to understand and utilize the data for analysis.

Depending on how data warehouses and marts were built, the data they contain may or may not be suitable for use in personalized advertising. Here are a few things that may get in the way of using this data:

- The data may be quite old. Many data warehouses were used primarily for historical analysis and reporting of customer activity and could be months or even quarters old. Using such data for personalized advertising would be challenging because this type of advertising really should use up-to-date (and in some cases real-time) information about customers.

- The data will likely not be tied to online customer identification. This is usually a cookie (or advertising ID for mobile users). This is critical because when a user sees an advertisement from the brand, he or she is essentially anonymous to the advertisement unless the advertisement can read ad cookies and match each cookie with customer data that is contained in the data warehouse. This is a step that needs to be completed before the data can be used for personalized marketing.

- The data may not be integrated across various customer touch points. For example, loyalty programs often have data that is not integrated with the rest of the customer data, and so a simple check to see if a customer belongs to the brand's loyalty program may not be possible in a single data warehouse.

- The data warehouse will not usually have the ability to integrate other social and mobile and/or third-party data that may be useful in developing a personalization profile for a user. This would limit its usage for personalization of advertising.

- The data warehouse will often contain personally identifiable information (PII), and having such information in a data store that will be used for marketing could be risky because it might inadvertently be made available outside the company or could provide an easy target to hack.

- Latency issues may exist with retrieving the data dynamically. Data warehouses were primarily designed for offline reporting, where a report or query could take a few seconds to even a few hours. For a personalized advertisement, a query needs to be completed in a few milliseconds

Developing a Personalization Data Store (PDS)

In many cases, given the reasons listed previously, it may be best to just start from scratch and build a database for the specific purpose of personalization.

The first thing to consider when building a personalization data store (PDS) is that it will be very large, and so Big Data technology should ideally be used to do it. Big Data technology refers to database, storage, and caching technology that enables large amounts of data to be stored and retrieved rapidly in real time.

Unlike traditional database technology, which was designed to efficiently store and retrieve traditional forms of data, Big Data technology is optimized for much higher volumes of data.

Big Data Technology

The primary premise of Big Data technology is that the workload and storage functions of a database can be distributed across many server systems, which means the database can be scaled almost infinitely by simply adding more servers, or "nodes," to the system.

The most popular of these systems is known as Hadoop. Hadoop is an open source system that is managed by the Apache Software Foundation. The Hadoop system primarily consists of a distributed file storage system called HDFS (which manages the actual storage and retrieval of data across nodes) and Hadoop MapReduce, which is a system for parceling out jobs to be executed on the data.

With so much data stored in a single system, what happens if the database goes down? Thankfully, the designers of Hadoop have actually thought about that. The Hadoop system is highly fault tolerant and simply never really will go down as there is no single point of failure of the database system. In large implementations of Hadoop, it is not unusual to have several thousand such nodes, and on any given day, several of them may fail, but the system will continue to operate, simply switching the tasks to other nodes. Yahoo, Facebook, Google, and Amazon all use some forms of the Hadoop system for storage and retrieval of the massive amounts of data they handle. Facebook recently announced that it was adding as much as half a petabyte of data each day to its Hadoop-based database system.

Hadoop is not the easiest system when it comes to retrieving data as it was not built to understand some of the common query languages, like SQL. The Apache Software Foundation has made available another open source framework called Apache Hive that can help you get the job done by building a SQL-like layer on top of the Hadoop system so that it is easier to query data out of the Hadoop system.

Creating a PDS

A PDS should contain any data that would be useful for the personalization of marketing campaigns and specifically for advertising.

While an exhaustive list is well beyond the scope of this book, the types of data that probably belongs in a PDS are the following:

- Website activity of the user/customer
- Purchase history
- Loyalty program details (e.g., points, miles, status, how long the user has been a customer)
- Social media data (i.e., posts to the brand's social media site, likes or pins of items on the brand's pages)
- Mobile application usage data
- Third-party data (which will reside in a third-party data store, but references can be kept in this data store)
- Second-party data (i.e., data from marketing partners) that may provide valuable predictors of purchase behavior

Together, these types of data enable the brand to build a 360-degree profile of a customer that can be used effectively to personalize marketing for the user.

As this data is being set up, it is important to ensure that the PDS does not contain any personally identifiable information (PII) on the user. This is important for two reasons: to avoid inadvertently disclosing any PII in marketing campaigns and also as a safeguard against hackers who would have a wealth of information if they gained access to this data source and could create major PR problems for the brand and lots of headaches for their customers. Kinds of PII to specifically look for and eliminate are names, Social Security numbers, detailed home addresses (city/zip may be useful for personalization, but anything more detailed will be a source of problems), phone numbers, user IDs, Facebook or Twitter names/handles, and names of friends or mentions of names of friends in feeds, posts, blogs, etc.

One way to ensure that data without any PII can still be tied together to form an individual profile is to use a new anonymous user identification key. This should ideally be a numeric key that does not contain any PII. As tempting as it may be to use a concatenation of name and Social Security numbers, it should rather be a completely random and unique number assigned to each user profile. We can refer to this key as a unique marketing user ID (UMUI).

This key then needs to be tied to a set of external identifiers, which will allow the user to be identified externally, and mapped to this internal user identifier. The external identifiers would be things like mobile advertiser IDs and special keys in user cookies. The UMUI should be the primary key by which all the attributes of the user are tied together within the PDS.

The data schema in the PDS needs to be designed differently than the data warehouse(s) from which the data may have been extracted because it needs to be designed for efficient retrieval and presentation to the dynamic ad serving platform and other personalization platforms in real time.

Certain dynamic ad platforms (like Jivox) do their own storage and caching of the relevant subsets of user data so that retrieval and usage of the data in real time are not hampered. In this case, latency may not be much of an issue. However, if data is being directly used in rendering an advertisement, the PDS architecture needs to factor in latency and availability.

Data Cleansing and Translation

One of the big challenges with data in general and specifically data that was not originally collected to be used for marketing is that the data usually needs a lot of reformatting and translation before it can be used effectively for personalized advertising.

CRM and other customer data systems are notorious for encoding data using cryptic codes in order to save space in their databases. For example, a customer loyalty database might use codes like Z1, Z2, and Z3 to indicate the levels of loyalty of the customers. This, of course, is complete gibberish to someone who has no idea about those codes, so often a significant amount of work needs to go into cleaning up and reformatting this data so it can be used in the PDS.

Software for such cleanup has been available for many years from companies like Informatica (my first company), Oracle, and IBM, but it can be a bit of work to get all the data cleaned up and ready for use. The good news is that all this is a one-time activity, and when it's completed, all the new data coming into these systems simply trickles into the PDS translated and ready for use.

Data Schema for a PDS

A PDS has to have a well-thought-out schema so that the key elements of data that can and should be used for personalization are available in the database.

Rather than have just raw data, for example, from a product sales database or website, the data needs to be processed first to make it easier to make personalization decisions from it. For example, rather than create just a raw list of products the customer has purchased, it may be more useful to have a list of categories; for example, for shoes you might use categories such as Running, Tennis, and Soccer, which would indicate the sporting activities the user likes to engage in. Further, it might be useful to know whether someone purchased discounted shoes only or opted for the newest and most expensive versions.

It might also be valuable to have in a PDS purchasing data that is aggregated to see if users are in the top, middle, or bottom brackets of spending; whether they are seasonal spenders or spend through the year; etc.

A PDS should be viewed not as the only source of data but rather as an encyclopedia of sorts, where information about a user profile is organized and categorized so it can be used in decision making related to personalization. Most real-time data being used for personalization will not be in the PDS (but may eventually be updated into the PDS to continue to build the profile) as it may need to be used for decision making immediately and is very transactional in nature. For example, if a user selected a particular shoe but did not purchase it, that data directly from the site cookie should be used for personalization (armed, perhaps, with data from the PDS that indicates the color preference of the user, based on historical purchases).

Here are some guidelines (by no means comprehensive) for the kinds of data and aggregations it may make sense to include in a PDS:

- Website activity
  - Cookie linkage
  - Browsed product categories

- Purchased product categories
- Ratio of browsed to purchased products
- Purchase history (offline and online)
  - Product categories
  - Annual spend
  - Spend type (nondiscounted new, bargain discounted, etc.)
  - Seasonality
  - Preferences (color, size, etc.)
- Loyalty program
  - Tenure
  - Category (gold, platinum, etc.)
  - Trend (more or less loyal recently)
  - Points balance (miles, points, etc.)
  - Amenities balance (i.e., what amenities could they take advantage of that they haven't)
- Social media data
  - Liked pages
  - Posted/pinned to page
  - Social media type
  - Post frequency
- Mobile application data
  - Usage frequency (hourly, daily, weekly, monthly)
  - Transactions performed
  - Purchases
  - Time spent
  - Preferences data (colors, categories, etc.)
  - Browsed to purchased
- Third-party data
  - Links to third-party data
  - Copies of third-party data for quick matches

- Second-party data
  - Links to second-party data
  - Copies of second-party data, where necessary

Other Data Sources and Derivative Data

Third-party data warrants a detailed discussion. Many data providers, such as data management platforms (DMPs), provide rich data sets that they have aggregated and offer to advertisers. Such data should be integrated with a brand's own first-party data, and the brand's PDS should be the integration point between the two. "Cookie sync" is a method that is typically used to accomplish this, whereby a link is created between the brand's first-party cookie and the third-party cookie. This then allows the brand's first-party data to be integrated with and used in conjunction with third-party data. It leads to a large number of data variables and a much broader data profile and significantly better personalization than can be achieved with just first-party data. While the cost of such data is always a consideration, given the explosion of data from many different sources and as data continues to get commoditized in the market, the price of data is starting to significantly decline.

Second-party data is a category that is often overlooked. While third-party data refers to data from a data aggregator, such as a DMP, second-party data is data obtained from direct sources, such as marketing partners. For example, airlines, car rental companies, and hotel chains all cater to the same customer and yet don't really compete with one another. Data agreements between such companies could significantly augment data for each of these providers. For example, American Airlines does not know about all the travelers who travel frequently to Miami, but Hertz does. Likewise, Hertz does not know about travelers who travel to Miami via American Airlines but use another car rental company. Similar synergies exist between real estate companies and insurance companies, between auto companies and insurance companies, etc.

Second-party data agreements can often just be "fair trade" agreements with no cost (i.e., you give me your data, and I'll give you mine).

Such data, of course, has to be anonymized between the parties so as not to compromise users' privacy.

Even the most sophisticated brands often have only partial data on their customers because many of their customers don't visit their websites or use their apps. If a brand has retail outlets, it may have some data, but that data is difficult to tie to the user's digital presence. Such incomplete data leads to incomplete personalization. For many brands, the number of customers who engage directly with them may be relatively small compared to the number of people who see their advertisements. Digital advertising campaigns for even midsize brands serve up tens of millions of ad impressions; unless they are an online-only retailer, the number of visitors to their site is typically much smaller.

One technique used to overcome this issue is referred to as "look-alike modeling," which involves using algorithms to fill out profiles by using inference techniques. It goes something like "If A likes what B likes and B likes X, then A must like X." This is an oversimplified version of look-alike modeling but captures the essence of the technique.

Look-alike modeling is used to try to locate audiences with behavioral patterns similar to those of people who are definitely in the intended audience. For example, automobile brands often tend to look for *auto intenders*, or people who have exhibited clear indications that they are in the market for an automobile. However, if an automaker targeted only such audiences, it would be challenged with not getting enough reach for its campaigns. Also, it would not be able to get its message to folks who may be in the market for an automobile but may not be exhibiting some of the same behavioral activities as the auto intenders. Look-alike modeling may be able to expand this audience by expanding this universe in two primary ways:

- **Multivariate analysis:** The decision to label someone as an auto intender may not be based on a single variable but on a number of variables. This could be as many as a few to several hundred variables, depending on the sophistication of the algorithms used. One way to extend the auto intender universe is to allow for inclusion of people exhibiting fewer of the behaviors typically exhibited by auto intenders.

- **Correlation:** This is a more typical way to look at the overall universe of behaviors auto intenders exhibit, including behaviors not necessarily associated with buying a car (e.g., visiting college tuition loan sites may indicate researching college savings plans). The behavioral attributes to pick, of course, should be the ones that are shared by a larger pool of the auto intenders and therefore may be indicative of an attribute that is an indirect attribute that others may have without having the primary attributes associated with being in the market for a car.

Amazon very early on used such techniques, referred to as "collaborative filtering," to try to guess what else you might be interested in. So, for example, if you purchase a book on gardening, and Amazon's data shows that a large percentage of people who buy books on gardening also tend to buy travel books, then you will see travel book recommendations start to appear when you log in. Sometimes this is puzzling for users as there is no apparent direct correlation between people who like to garden and people who like to travel. However, with the benefit of very large data sets and a large set of powerful computers, Amazon is able to make such correlations that may not be very obvious and yet are very valuable.

It may also be helpful to use all this data to create aggregate categories for each profile, such as loyal, growing, new, declining, etc. Other super-categories could be spend amounts, locations (travel), other interests (perhaps based on third-party data), etc.

The data should be as recent as possible because personalized advertising is most effective when the data is near real time. Folks complain about personalized advertisements that continue to show them products they already own. This tends to happen when the system uses data indicating that the user once browsed that product and the data did not immediately get updated once the purchase was completed.

Inferences and Predictive Modeling

Once the basic data infrastructure is in place for a PDS, it may be useful to take things a step further—into the realm of inferences and predictive modeling. The idea behind inferences and predictive modeling is that by processing large amounts of data related to customer behavior and interactions with a brand, we can start to make inferences and predictively model what a customer is likely to do in the future. For example, it is quite possible based on purchase history to model age, gender, etc., and so inferences and predictions about when a user is likely to need certain products can be made based on his or her past purchases.

Predictive modeling requires expertise in the field of data mining and analytics—and increasingly in machine learning and artificial intelligence as well. These disciplines can help marketers get much better at inferring or predicting customer behavior, and the resulting data will be invaluable to personalization efforts.

The more data inputs to predictive modeling, the better the outcomes will be. For example, recording the local weather conditions at the time of a transaction, the time of day, other events that might have been going on, and even what's in the news can help predictive modeling algorithms find patterns that humans cannot find, given the vast amounts of data involved.

Determining under what conditions users have in the past purchased products can be invaluable in personalization efforts as personalization can rely on the wisdom of crowds to help determine what would work best for a specific individual.

Research shows that as much as 35% to 60% of Amazon purchases come from recommendations made using purchase history of millions of shoppers. This kind of inference is not limited to the retail industry alone, even though that is probably where it has been used the most. Netflix uses such technology to make recommendations about what to watch, including emailing a user to say that a new movie that he or she "may be interested in watching" is now available on Netflix.

Similarly, the hotel industry could use such predictive methods to know when to offer holiday vs. business travel messaging to a user, based on patterns of when people tend to plan vacations and maybe even destinations, using location information from the usage of the brand's mobile app.

Machine learning techniques, which often are used for optimizing campaigns, can also be used to develop predictive models for better personalization. Predicting what triggers cause a consumer to purchase is extraordinarily difficult, given that there are often many variables involved. It is challenging to determine when a consumer may be ready to make a purchase, and it is also challenging to determine likely buyers of a product or likely influencers of a purchase. Handling all this difficult and bewildering stuff is exactly what machine learning technologies are designed to do.

Machine learning technologies are designed to take very large numbers of variables and their associated data and outcomes and come up with a "formula" for determining what data can predict the outcomes. Machine learning algorithms usually require vast amounts of data as input and tremendous amounts of computing power in order to process the data.

Big Data: A Process, Not a Database

Big Data is not simply about collecting data and building a database but about changing the way marketing is done to make it much more data centric than it has historically been. Personalization enables marketers to more effectively harness all the data they have had for many years into an application that will lift sales and create greater brand loyalty.

Big Data should therefore be viewed not as a destination but as a journey, where processes for collecting, aggregating, and enhancing data are continuously improved on with constant measurement of results to make sure these efforts are paying off.

Other Data Integration Technologies

In addition to developing their own data capabilities, many brands are also starting to look to commercial technology and data vendors to provide them with other data to help extend their data capabilities.

Several breakthroughs in data management technology have made it possible to use data to deliver higher performance to advertising campaigns. The technologies themselves are very simple in nature and have come about because of the Internet's tremendous ability to let systems that don't know much about each other communicate via

APIs. Traditional technologies and software packages were incredibly poor at communicating with each other—hence the difficulty in integrating and using the data for advertising.

Two key breakthrough technologies have emerged in the past several years that have made it possible to solve some of the key issues with traditional data management for marketing: cookie/ID sync and cookie-based preference profiles. All the data collected using these two methods is completely anonymous and can be accomplished without using any personally identifiable information.

Cookie/ID Sync

Cookie sync sounds very sophisticated but is really a very simple mechanism that allows different collectors of data to talk to each other without knowing about or exchanging personally identifiable information about the consumer. Cookie sync does, as it sounds like it would, use cookies, which enable websites to "remember" you without knowing who you are.

Let's consider an example. Say that Angie loves cars and often visits Car and Driver to learn about the newest cars and car-related facts. Angie is, of course, telling the site a lot about what she likes. The site can store this information in a cookie in her browser and then use what it knows about Angie's habits to tailor content to her. This technology has been around for almost as long as websites have been around, and the data involved is referred to as first-party data. While the data says a lot about Angie's interest in cars, it doesn't say much more. In fact, it doesn't even know that Angie is female. (In fact, going by simple demographic probabilities for automobile sites, one might incorrectly conclude that she is a male visitor.)

It turns out that Angie is also a frequent visitor to Elle.com, which can with a significantly higher degree of certainty conclude that Angie is female and also has a lot of data about her interests as a woman.

The big problem, as discussed earlier, is how to combine the two data sets to better market to Angie.

Cookie sync technology allows the data from Car and Driver to be correlated to data from Elle.com to determine that both data sets describe the same individual and can therefore be used to build a "profile" of the person. This is done using intermediary technology platforms referred to as DMPs (discussed later in this chapter).

The way cookie sync works online is simple, as we'll see with Angie as an example: A website has a *tag* that contains some code that drops a cookie in Angie's browser when she visits the site and simultaneously makes a redirect URL call to a DMP, telling it that it has registered Angie and discloses a unique ID for her. The redirect allows the DMP to look for its own cookie to see if it knows Angie from elsewhere; if it doesn't, it will assign a unique identifier to her and pass that back to the site, which can now record that identifier. So essentially what has happened is that Car and Driver and the DMP have exchanged identifiers so that the next time Angie shows up on Car and Driver, the DMP immediately knows she is the same person it saw last time; in the meantime, if Angie has also visited Elle.com, the DMP now has even more information about her than it had last time: It now knows she is female.

Cookie sync is relatively easy to do between online first-party data stores. But it doesn't work between online stores and brick-and-mortar stores. Connections between online and offline activity continue to be a challenge from a data integration perspective. Let's look further at Angie's activities to see ways by which that could be accomplished.

Now consider that Angie also went to Costco to shop one weekend. She bought a few car accessories and other items at the physical store. Costco probably has a record of all this data, but the problem is that Costco's CRM system has no knowledge of Angie's online activity—only what happened in the store. When Angie completes her purchase in the physical store, she provides her Costco membership card, which has her unique Costco ID. Let's now say Angie then goes to Costco's website and registers when she makes some other purchases and checks out: She has identified herself and allowed Costco to cookie her and use her login to identify and match that with the data in its CRM system so that Angie's offline purchase data is now connected with her online purchase data.

This same process can occur even if the online and offline data collection happen across two retailers because the "common key"—that is, a key that exists in both data sets (e.g., last name or credit card number)—can be used to synchronize the data.

Now all that has to happen is that Costco's CRM database (which knows Angie's Costco cookie ID) is synced with the DMP's data about her activity at Car and Driver and Elle.com.

Keep in mind that the DMP still does not know who Angie is but simply knows that she is an anonymous person who loves cars, is probably female, and likes to bargain shop and perhaps has a family (that can consume the giant packages of food she purchases at Costco).

One of the challenges with the URL method of syncing is that it is ideal for synchronizing identities but not so great for syncing data. Because data would have to be exchanged within milliseconds during an ad call or when the user is on a website, sometimes significant latencies can be introduced if a data sync is also attempted during a cookie sync. Therefore, many first-party data providers and DMPs have developed "server-to-server" integrations. As the name implies, these are APIs that allow the data sources and DMPs to exchange actual data in volume outside the cookie sync calls so as not to slow down the cookie sync process.

Some data providers and DMPs also do "batch" processing of data, where large data sets are synchronized overnight to make sure all systems stay in sync.

Server-to-server synchronization is key in powering digital ads because the decisions to serve a particular ad or variation of messaging have to be made within milliseconds, and so the closer the data is to the decisioning engine, the more likely it is to deliver the ad and message on time.

Cookie-Based Preference Profiles

Many brands, especially consumer brands, have a large number of their customers and prospects visit their websites. Many brands have realized that the best way to capture preferences and interests of customers is to record their activities on a brand's website and use that information to build a profile of each user.

The activities on a brand's website can say a lot about a consumer. For example, for a financial services brand, the website activity could help understand the age bracket; for example, older customers are more likely to browse retirement products, while younger ones may be browsing college savings funds. In the automobile industry, this kind of site data can tell brands what car model you may be in the market for, what features you are interested in (e.g., luggage space vs. handling), and even what your favorite car color is.

E-commerce sites have long used preference data to showcase "other products you might like" by matching up what you browsed for with other users' browsing data to find products others like you also browsed for and use that to recommend purchases. This data can also be used to recommend products using dynamic/personalized ads.

Challenges on Mobile Devices

The techniques described so far in this chapter have been very useful in display advertising for desktop computers. However, these methods have suddenly become very challenging on mobile devices. Several constraints on mobile devices make it very difficult to use data collected using the above methods in marketing:

- Cookies are problematic on mobile devices. Some mobile browsers do not allow the use of third-party cookies and allow only first-party cookies or no cookies at all.

- Cookies dropped in a web browser environment on a user's desktop are not visible in the user's mobile browser environment so that cookie data cannot be used. The reverse is also true: A cookie dropped in a mobile environment cannot be used on a desktop.

- Even within mobile devices, no data can be shared between a mobile device's browser environment and the mobile application environment on that same device.

Mobile devices have therefore now erected "walls" between the various environments the user operates in, and this has made it challenging to collect and use such data for marketing.

Due to the challenges with cookies on mobile devices, Apple and other mobile device manufacturers have introduced other "identifiers" that could be used to identify a user (without using PII data) for the purpose of personalizing advertising. These identifiers, called *advertising IDs* or *ad IDs*, can be used to identify a user (or, more precisely, a user's device) uniquely. The issue with such identifiers is that they can be accessed only within mobile applications—not within mobile web browsing—and so this kind of identification is challenging.

Other techniques, such as browser and other "device" signatures, are increasingly being used by advertising technologies to more precisely identify users. A common technique is to tie together several devices, using the fact that they often are used on the same network IP addresses (e.g., at the user's home). With signatures, too, it is not a single piece of data that uniquely identifies a user but rather several pieces of data, often gathered by several different data collection methods, to build a profile of the user. Many of these methods are not 100% accurate; it is not unusual for accuracy levels to be in the range of 65% to 80%, which is considered good for mobile identification. Large publishers have been able to do more precise cross-device identification using login information.

Mobile user identification is becoming a very big focus area for personalized advertising as consumers increasingly spend more browsing and shopping time on mobile devices than on their desktops.

For personalization efforts, many data signals do not really require identification of the user at all but rather the user's environment. For example, triggers based on weather, geography, stock market, location, etc., can be used easily on mobile devices and do not require cookies or other identification technology in order to be used.

Data Management Platforms (DMPs)

We talked a little bit about DMPs earlier, in the context of synchronizing data, but you may still be wondering what exactly a DMP is. Simply put, a DMP is a piece of software coupled with a very large, fast, and efficient database management system that enables data to be synchronized across a wide variety of data sources and enables advertisers to create audience segments that can be targeted with specific ads or messaging.

A DMP cannot operate by itself as it needs various sources and users of data to be useful. So in some ways, it is like a hub or air traffic control system that collects data from many sources and makes sure data across these systems stays synchronized.

DMPs also enable advertisers to create "audience segments." Depending on the capabilities of the DMP software as well as data licensing partnerships, DMPs can have very basic data sets or very sophisticated and detailed data about individuals. The "newness" of the data, or how recently the data was collected, may also vary significantly between DMPs.

Most DMPs, as part of their data agreements with their customers (e.g., publishers), also collect data from those customers' traffic. So, for example, if a DMP vendor has an agreement to provide data to a particular website, it will also collect data about visitors to that website, thus continuing to enrich the data, making it more recent and relevant to other customers. Similarly, when large ad networks or exchanges use DMPs, they also provide cookie data back to the DMPs, and so the data available on an individual user can rapidly grow and become more complete very quickly.

Some DMPs also have data agreements with offline data providers, such as retailers. Here the online cookie data can often be synchronized with offline data to provide a more complete picture of the user to the DMP.

Another technique often used to make correlations between disparate data sets is to use look-alike modeling. As discussed earlier in this chapter, the idea here is that sometimes correlations can be made between audience segments, so new segments can be defined by simply finding correlations between known audience segments.

An example of such correlations could be that people who purchase gardening products would also likely be people who would purchase organic products, people who purchased airline tickets recently may be in the market for hotels, etc. Look-alike modeling enables DMPs to build profiles of people for whom they have only partial information.

17

Content Development for Personalization

The drive to personalize advertising does not come without a cost. In order to provide high-quality personalized communication with users, a brand has to invest in developing messaging and content that are specific to the brand.

At first this might seem daunting, and it is certainly a big departure from the single jingle or copy version that got blasted out to everyone, regardless of their interests. But it does pay off to develop high-quality content and messaging that will really enable the brand to engage with users.

Most brands now have content teams that produce content for their social media presence. This discipline, often referred to as "content marketing," was primarily used to "earn" media, and it has been sometimes criticized as being hard to justify. For example, a brand might have spent several hundred thousand dollars producing high-quality video content and then try to get users to view it on YouTube or Facebook. The fact that only about 2% of videos uploaded to YouTube get more that 100,000 views is enough to make any marketer wonder about investing in YouTube videos. Likewise, content posted on Facebook, even when paid for, has very low reach numbers: It is likely that a piece of content posted by a brand will reach only 16% of its followers organically. All this makes it very hard to justify production of content just for earned media and small reach numbers.

If, however, brands consider what all that valuable content can do to paid media advertising, the numbers get really interesting. Brands are already spending quite a bit on paid media advertising, and so integrating all that paid media with this content can significantly increase the ROI for content production.

This model of using content produced for earned media in paid media essentially serves to provide highly personalized ad experiences, producing engagement in the larger numbers of people that paid media tends to reach.

The idea of introducing content into paid media advertising is also very relevant for brands that sponsor sporting, entertainment, and other events. Liquor brands, auto brands, and other consumer brands often sponsor sporting or other local and regional events. Often a lot of content is produced at or for these events, and so the idea of personalizing advertising would be to take that content and deliver it in paid media. For example, if Mercedes were sponsoring a local golf tournament, it could personalize the Mercedes ads in that area with content from the event (e.g., photos with the winner of the tournament, pictures of the winner of the giveaway, etc.). This kind of "in the moment" marketing pays off tremendously as users tend to relate well to local events. It also makes the brand appear smart and aware of what is going on.

Producing content specific for user segments can pay off significantly. For example, an auto manufacturer could make an SUV more appealing to skiers by showing footage from the local mountain ski resorts and/or images with the SUV going up the mountain with ski gear. At the same time, in a different part of the country, the content might be about going camping or to a lake. Developing messaging for different subsegments of users takes some effort but can pay off as the advertising becomes much more targeted and relevant to each user.

All this often brings up the question of who should be responsible for all this development of content and messaging and also ensuring that the right content reaches the right user segments.

Creative agencies often view their roles as just coming up with clever tag lines, visually appealing images, videos, etc., and not really as being data, content, or targeting experts. Media teams at agencies, on the other hand, do worry about target audience segments and so on but often don't have the skills or resources to determine and develop content and messaging for audience segments for the brand.

This kind of effort is increasingly being undertaken by the brands themselves, usually leaning on or expanding their social media content teams to produce content and messaging for personalizing their paid media campaigns.

Many brands have set up newsroom-style teams that are constantly developing content and making content available for use in social media and other earned media. Brands have a great opportunity to do this, and several have used their team and pool of constantly produced assets to deliver dynamic and personalized ads. When an event occurs that the brand can and should have a voice for, this team rapidly comes up with messaging and assets that can then be "published" into earned media and incorporated as dynamic content and messaging in advertisements.

This style of advertising shows the brand as being progressive, in touch with consumer sentiment, and adding value to consumers rather than being disruptive and annoying in a quest to sell more products.

The content itself can be of various forms, and creativity with content is as much about creating visual appeal as emotional appeal. A few categories might be

- **Entertaining:** If brands want to become more like media publishers, they have to act like them and make their content entertaining and engaging. Content should not always be a plug for the brand but rather should focus on engaging the user. Entertaining content always gets users to engage, and their perception of the brand gets tied to that, too. For example, Virgin America produced an in-flight video that was one of the most fun pieces of serious messaging there could have been. In-flight safety videos, which are monitored and regulated by the FAA, are about as serious as it gets, and yet the Virgin marketing team found a way to make theirs entertaining and fun. My kids went to YouTube after we landed and watched it so many times, they had it memorized and turned it into a skit.

- **Educational:** Brands should strive to make content educational. For example, if you are an outdoor brand, you could share tips on avoiding allergies while outdoors. Will that directly help sell more hiking boots? Not necessarily, but consumers are more likely to purchase hiking boots from a brand that they perceive cares about their health and safety than from one that doesn't.

- **Useful:** When a consumer is interested in the product being advertised, content that provides more details especially tailored to the individual also creates great engagement. For example, a male consumer would likely be more interested in the power and features of an automobile than necessarily the fact that it can carry five kids and their soccer gear in the rear. Rather than expect the user to click on the ad, arrive at a landing page, and then try to find the relevant content the specific consumer is likely to consume, why not curate and present the content to the consumer based on his or her profile data? An ad for baking mixes may benefit from recipe videos tailored to the holiday occasion (e.g., Christmas cookies, Thanksgiving pies, etc.).

User-generated content is sometimes useful, and working with it can pay off—especially for consumer brands, where user participation can help drive engagement as the content is often shared via social media and can become viral.

Data used to drive personalization can also be used to intelligently serve up relevant content. For example, for a brand targeting sports enthusiasts, like GoPro, each person to whom the ad is served may be engaged in a different sport; since GoPro caters to sports enthusiasts of all kinds, it is often difficult for GoPro to determine what sporting content to feature in its advertisements. By using a powerful combination of data about its users and content, GoPro can create a very engaging set of advertisements. The way this would work is that GoPro would identify a set of data signals that determine what sport a user is interested in (e.g., from their own website or shared content engagement or third-party data sources). Once the data signals have been identified, the content has to be categorized into the same sports categories (e.g., biking, skiing, canoeing, etc.), and then using a dynamic ad-serving platform, mapping rules can be set up to match each user profile (i.e., biker, skier) to the appropriate content.

Since GoPro produces and sources a lot of content from its users, this kind of content can be set up as a feed into the advertisements, where the feed is switched based on the user profile and always contains a set of content fed into the ad in real time.

Investing in content development enables brands to drive higher levels of engagement, not only in social and earned media but increasing at scale using paid media. Great content drives engagement much more than any clever ad copy can and should be the foundation of any ad personalization efforts.

18

Technology for Developing Data-Driven Advertisements

Several pieces of technology come into play to bring a data-driven personalized ad campaign to reality.

Ad Development and Production the Old Way

The process of developing ads for personalized ad campaigns is very different from the traditional methods of ad production. With nondynamic ads, of course, the process is very linear and simple. An ad gets coded, tested, and instrumented with appropriate tracking, and then it is launched.

Many dynamic ad campaigns initially tried to use this same process and tools, but the number of possible variations of creative very quickly overwhelmed the creative production and QA teams. For campaigns with a minimal number of creative variations (say 3 to 10), this process could work, and it often did with DCO, where the goal was to test and compare a few creative ideas.

With personalized advertising campaigns, though, the number of creative variants can be very large, often running into the thousands. Indeed, that is the point of personalized advertising: An ad can and should be personalized almost down to an individual.

Several platforms have tried to address the issue of scaling production by using templates. With such platforms, a base template has placeholders for assets, and the assets are retrieved, usually via an XML feed, and rendered in the placeholder slot. This approach, while a lot more scalable than building hundreds or thousands of ads, has issues in that it is often unpredictable in terms of the size and format of the assets that may have to be rendered in the template. This often triggers lots of code changes in the templates, leading to a very cumbersome process for editing and fixing such issues as images or text overlapping or being cut off.

The code- and template-based process for ad production also creates a lot of issues with reporting. If multiple ads are created, then hundreds and sometimes thousands of ads have to be instrumented with analytics/reporting tags, and that can be a very time-consuming and error-prone process.

Tagging code-based ads for reporting is also made more complex by the fact that the tracking pixels or tags need to report back things like creative variants and other conversion codes and attributes that may not be known until just before campaign launch. Also, sometimes changes occur in such tracking codes, which in turn triggers a large number of code changes to each ad to ensure that the new codes are used.

With code templates, the same problem exists in a different way: With code templates, the tracking often needs to be implemented in the template itself, and so such templates often cannot report the kinds of detailed data needed for dynamic personalized ads since they don't record information about the individual assets that are varying in each ad.

Clearly, a new approach is needed to create and deliver personalized ads at scale.

Dynamic Ads, Dynamic Ad Platform

In order to deliver dynamic personalized advertising campaigns at scale, a whole new approach is required, utilizing technology that can enable such ad campaigns to scale both from production and serving standpoints.

The problem with the prevalent ad production process described above is that the tools and processes were built assuming a static ad that remains the same throughout the campaign. A creative person came up with a concept, a developer coded the ad, they went back and forth a few times (sometimes more than a few times), and once the ad was finalized, the campaign was launched and usually remained the same throughout. This model simply does not work for personalized ads as it assumes a one-time linear process of ad development and serving.

The ideal model for dynamic personalized advertising is a more dynamic publishing model rather than a linear one-time model. The publishing model allows any content in the ad to be changed on-the-fly, based on data signals that can constantly change, depending on who and where the ad is being delivered to.

Before we look at what a dynamic ad platform would look like, let's first dissect a dynamic ad. Each personalized ad, in general, has two key sets of components—a set of components that don't change from one version to the other (e.g., logo, skin, etc.) and another set of components that vary, sometimes for each ad that gets served. Separating these components and managing them separately are key to scaling the process. It also turns out that this is key to tracking and reporting. This leads us to the first key piece of a dynamic ad platform: a component architecture/model.

Component-Based Model for Ad Content

A component-based model for ad content allows each part of a dynamic/personalized ad to exist as a standalone entity, so it can be swapped out without impacting the rest of the ad. An ad component model allows marketers to develop ads in a modular way without hard coding assets into an ad, thereby making the assets easy to swap.

Every ad contains a number of assets (e.g., images, videos, animations, etc.). To ensure these assets can be dynamically swapped, an ad component can be defined to describe each of the assets. The ad component contains metadata (metadata is data about data or objects) that describes the asset (i.e., what kind of asset it is) and its properties or attributes. The metadata may also contain information on how the asset should be rendered in the ad.

The assets in an ad are often arranged in a *layout* in the ad; a *layout* defines the relative positioning of the assets of the ad to each other. For example, a logo might be at the bottom right and a video in the center of the ad. These assets often also have to be arranged in layers within an ad; *layers* are the vertical relative positions of the components in an ad. For example, an animation may be in the same position in the layout as a video, so the layer would determine whether the video is above or below the animation if both are rendered in the ad.

An advertisement therefore consists of a set of components as well as a layout, which defines how the components are placed relative to each other. Finally, *actions* define what happens when a user clicks or taps on any part of the ad.

In a dynamic ad, all these components are described using metadata rather than being hard coded in the ad. The metadata simply describes how the components are supposed to appear relative to each other and how they are supposed to interact with each other.

Each asset has several properties. For example, a video asset has properties related to the kind of video file it is (e.g., mov, flv, mp4, etc.), size, aspect ratio, etc. These properties are described in the metadata of that ad component.

Here is a sample of a JSON descriptor of such a component model for various components:

```
{
"interactionIdentifier": "asset102",
"icon": "http://jivoxdevassets.cdn.com/asset/2014/12/496-0-
aim5489230b04313.png",
"label": "IMG_23092014_012329",
"data": null,
"iconFileName": "IMG_23092014_012329.png",
"urlFileName": null,
"iconDimension": "[1366,768]",
"assetDimension": null,
"origIconDimension": "[1366,768]",
"origAssetDimension": null,
"assetBgColor": null,
"iconBgColor": null,
"iconFileType": "image",
"autoPlay": null,
"iconGlowColor": null,
"isIconBgTransparent": null,
"isWatermarkLogo": null,
```

```
"fallbackImgURL": null,
"fallbackImgFileName": null,
"shareUrlType": null,
"shareMsg": null,
"fallbackType": null,
"fallbackWidgetSrc": null,
"fallbackWidgetURL": null,
"fallbackWidgetFileName": null,
"clickHandler": null,
"iconCustomEventQueryStr": null,
}
```

This kind of descriptor serves two purposes. First, the ad inherently knows how to render an asset that is described this way, and so if an asset (i.e., image, video, etc.) is dynamic, all it needs to do is read this metadata to know what to do with it. Second, it allows a third-party system that may be delivering assets dynamically (e.g., a product catalog) to use a "language" that the dynamic ad platform understands and knows how to render.

Sometimes an asset may be virtual; that is, the ad component representing the asset may simply point to where the asset can be dynamically obtained and then at runtime, the actual asset is fetched, based on how the virtual asset is defined.

Content Management System

In a dynamic ad, the component model just presented describes how to ensure that components are not hard coded or hard wired into the ad. This ensures that they can be swapped out easily. But a new problem crops up: When an ad was hard coded with its assets, the assets were part of the ad. Where do the assets live when they are not being rendered in the ad?

Let's say a dynamic ad had four different skins, representing the weather conditions hot, cold, warm, and cool. At any given time, only one weather condition will be true, and therefore only one skin will be active. So where do we put the rest of the assets?

A content management system (CMS) is a key component of a dynamic ad platform. CMSs originated in systems and tools used to develop websites where content had to be updated frequently (e.g., e-commerce sites with new products and pricing being swapped in all the time). Earlier website technology required developers to modify the code of the site whenever an asset had to change. Modern website platforms, though, have a built-in CMS, so an update to website content is a simple matter of updating assets in the CMS.

In a dynamic ad platform, a CMS serves a similar purpose in that it houses the components of an ad until they need to be rendered in the ad. This allows dynamic ads with hundreds or even thousands of variants of messaging, images, videos, etc., possible since a CMS technically has no limits on the number of assets it can store.

It is not necessary to house all assets that can dynamically appear in an ad in the ad platform's CMS. In fact, in many cases, the assets may not be known upfront because they are being dynamically generated and may themselves change. For example, if a retailer has a product catalog where the products are constantly changing (e.g., electronics), it may be best to retrieve the catalog dynamically rather than store it in the CMS. Such assets are often referred to as *virtual assets*. In these cases, the CMS simply has a reference to those assets and can dynamically fetch them from wherever they are when needed.

CMSs are often built with an underlying content delivery network (CDN). A CDN ensures that assets are distributed vastly across the Internet so that they can quickly be retrieved without significant delays. This is very critical technology for dynamic ads; without it, ads would take forever to render because the components of the ad would mostly be fetched dynamically.

A CDN works like this: The CDN provider has thousands of server systems with ample storage located around the globe. When a request for an asset is made by an ad, rather than fetch the asset from a centralized location, it is fetched from the nearest "edge" server, with minimal latency. This technology has been around since the advent of websites and is used by practically every website to ensure that site load times are quick, regardless of where in the world the user is located. The edge servers are constantly synchronized with the central, or "master," copy of the assets in order to ensure that any changes to the master are reflected immediately to the edge servers.

Ad Development Studio

A dynamic ad platform requires an ad development studio in order to design and define ad layouts and produce an ad. Unlike traditional ad development studios, which are primarily code based, dynamic ad development studios are component based; that is, instead of writing a lot of code to describe how the ad should render, this new kind of studio enables ad components to be laid out and their properties defined in terms of how and when they should render.

Dynamic ad development studios typically feature a drag-and-drop environment that allows components to be uploaded and laid out without requiring much or any code to be written. The user interface typically also has ways to define layers, animation, and actions for the components and also has an environment for previewing an ad to ensure that it visually represents the creative design of the ad. For dynamic ads, this preview function is critical because in several campaigns there could be hundreds or even thousands of creative variants, and so this would provide a scalable way to ensure that all versions can be reviewed and, if necessary, approved.

An ad development studio also typically ensures that the various static or dynamic components of an ad are automatically tagged for analytics. This means there is no need for a specific "tagging process," which with older platforms meant editing the Flash code of the ad and instrumenting each component with tracking code to report on whether the element was clicked on, etc. This process of tagging is not only cumbersome but also error prone, especially for personalized ads, where several hundred to several thousand creative variants could be rendered and so manual code-based tagging would be challenging to do.

Personalized Ad Design Considerations

A dynamic or personalized advertisement generally consists of design elements that don't change from one user to another and another set of elements that change based on the user the ad is being served to.

While designing personalized advertisements, it is critical to ensure that these elements are separated out in the design as it will make the production process much easier and less painful. This does not mean creating a rigid template that doesn't look very appealing to users but just simply separating the elements out and yet integrating the design elements so that the dynamic components appear integrated into the ad experience.

There are several key considerations to keep in mind when designing personalized advertisements. One is that the assets are dynamically replaced, and so it is critical that the design factor in the form and fit of these dynamic assets without making the advertisement look templated and boxy.

When assets are dynamically replaced, sizing and fit can be challenging. Take text fields, for example. In cases where text is used, text for each dynamic variant can be of different lengths, so the design needs to ensure that the longest of the text can fit into the space allocated in the ad for the text; it also needs to ensure that the shortest of the text doesn't look like it is floating like a rowboat in the ocean. Similarly, due to issues related to aspect ratio, images can look outright clumsy and pasted on if size considerations are not taken into account. Because of the standardized aspect ratios of video, video is usually not a problem when it comes to dynamic layouts and can be swapped in and out pretty easily.

Here again, a good ad production platform designed for dynamic advertisements makes a big difference because of its ability to dynamically resize and ensure that assets fit and are rendered correctly.

Integrating with Data Signals

As discussed earlier, the key element of personalized ads is the data signals that tell the ad platform what messages and assets to render to a particular user. Due to the wide variety of data signals available, one of the key capabilities a dynamic ad platform needs to have is the ability to integrate with a wide variety of data signals.

There are several ways dynamic data signals can be accessed or received. Here are a few of the common ones:

- **API/web service/URL redirect:** An API is often used for data that is constantly changing and so has to be checked at the time of delivery of the ad and cannot be predetermined. Examples of such data signals are weather and geographic data and financial/stock market/interest rates data. If an API is used, it is often a REST or SOAP API that will return XML data or JSON-formatted data. A URL redirect is a simpler form of integration that involves invoking a URL with some information in the URL that identifies the campaign or ad; the URL is redirected by the data source, and the redirect then contains the data signal(s) needed by the ad. This mechanism is often used by DMPs to return audience segment identification data.

- **Cookie or tracking tag:** Cookies and tracking tags are often used when the data signal is specific to a user since it is visible only to the user from whose browser it was dropped; it is not suitable for general data signals available to everyone. Cookies can be used, for example, to drop preference information about a user visiting a website selecting a product, a color preference, etc. This information can be recorded in a cookie when the user visits the site so that the ad can dynamically look up the cookie and serve a personalized version of the creative (e.g., a car ad where the color is one of the user-indicated preferences). The cookie gets dropped using what is often referred to as a *tracking tag* that is placed on the website that the user may visit. It is often placed inside another tag, called a *container tag*, that is a permanent tag on the advertiser's website that can accept other tracking tags dynamically; this means the advertiser's web page does not have to be edited each time a new tracking tag needs to be placed on the site.

- **Ad tag signal:** In certain ad serving and programmatic environments, the publisher side ad server or the DSP is often capable of inserting data signals into the ad tag for the dynamic advertisement. This is usually done via a macro that the DSP or publisher ad server recognizes and replaces with a value. Dynamic ad platforms can often read that value and then use it as a data signal to swap in the right assets. For example, DSPs can often insert data signals about audience segment, and that can be used to serve the correct dynamic assets into the ad for that audience segment.

Technology for Storing, Retrieving, and Managing Dynamic Assets/Content

Dynamic ad campaigns require the ability to process and render hundreds and even thousands of assets at scale. In general, assets can be predetermined and known ahead of time, or they can be dynamically created.

As an example of predetermined assets, think about an insurance company that has a database of agents. The company is using agent photos and addresses to customize ads for each geography in which the ad is served. While the number of agents could be several thousand, the data remains fairly constant and is predetermined (i.e., known before the campaign launches).

Dynamic assets are assets that may not be available until a particular event occurs. For example, a beer brand may sponsor a local beach event, and if the brand wants to use assets from that beach event, the assets of course are not available until the event occurs, and they become irrelevant once the event is over. These assets are completely dynamic and need to be uploaded and served immediately and dynamically.

For even a small number of assets (say more than five), hard-coding assets into an ad creates a lot of issues. First, the ad itself can become very heavy and have trouble loading; this is particularly an issue with ads rendering on mobile devices, where bandwidth constraints combined with a heavy ad could mean the ad doesn't even load or render.

A CMS, as described earlier in this chapter, is an elegant solution to the problem. The CMS stores the assets needed by an ad until they are ready to be rendered and ensures that the assets are served on demand.

Dynamic assets may be assets related to special offers, changing product catalogs, or true real-time marketing, where content may specifically and quickly be created to take advantage of something that just happened (e.g., the Oreos "You can still dunk in the dark" example showcased earlier).

For these kinds of dynamic assets, or assets not known up front, a number of methods can be used to deliver the assets to the ad, as described next.

Feed-Based Assets

Many websites, especially e-commerce sites, have their own CMS system. In-house content production teams also often use an in-house CMS that is distinct from the CMS used by the dynamic ad platform. In these cases, the assets can be delivered dynamically using the methods described in the following sections.

RSS Feeds

RSS stands for Really Simple Syndication; this standard, which has been available for quite some time, provides a quick and easy way for content to be accessed from one system to another. The standard essentially is a "feed" in which text and image elements can be delivered to a receiver system (e.g., the dynamic ad platform) from a publisher (e.g., a site's CMS). RSS feeds, while simpler and somewhat less flexible than other feed formats, have a significant benefit in that reading and rendering an RSS feed can be done without an agreement on both endpoints about the content in the feed. In other words, each feed element is expected to have an image, a description, a link, etc., so the receiver can read the elements and render them, regardless of where they are coming from.

Here is what an RSS feed looks like:

```
<rss xmlns:feedburner="http://rssnamespace.org/feedburner/
ext/1.0" version="2.0">
<channel>
          <title>ABEBC</title>
          <link>http://www.hotelcalifornia.com/</link>
          <description>HCalifornia </description>
          <pubDate>Tuesday, 4 June 2013 19:00:00 -0400</pubDate>
     <item>...</item>
     <item>...</item>
```

```
<item>
<title>Room - 507.00 USD</title>
        <link>http://www.hotelcalifornia.com/specials/
        hotel-deals.mi</link>
        <description>
        <![CDATA[
        1 King, Sofa bed, Mini-fridge, Wireless Internet,
        complimentary, Wired Internet, complimentary, Coffee/
        tea maker, 32in/81cm flatscreen TV. Tax is:50.70
        ]]>
        </description>
        <author>HCalifornia</author>
</item>
<item>...</item>
<item>...</item>
</channel>
</rss>
```

JSON Feeds

JavaScript Object Notation (JSON) is a much more sophisticated mechanism that allows more complex assets (e.g., video, animations, or pretty much anything) to be sent from one system to another. Each element in a JSON feed is a self-describing element that can have a list of attributes along with their values and perhaps URLs to assets. This model is very flexible and allows for a very wide variety of assets to be represented and delivered for personalization.

Here is what an element in a JSON feed looks like:

```
{"companyName":"Mona Smith Ins. Agency Inc.","phone":"(318) 235-
3299","imageURL":"http://playercdn.jivox.com/assets/1_person.
jpg","clickURL":"https://www.statesideinsurance.com/agent/US/LA/
Monroe/Mona-Smith-N4HGB21H000"}
```

Asset Databases

Asset databases can be as simple as files containing assets or links to assets, or they can be physical databases containing the assets. Asset databases are ideal for integrating with much older systems that may not support RSS or JSON directly as ways of dynamically retrieving assets.

Asset databases also provide a lot of scale, since there is technically no limit to the number of assets that can be stored and very efficiently retrieved when needed. Typically, asset databases are created by processing a set of asset and other descriptor files that are downloaded from a secure site owned by the brand. This allows assets to be updated periodically and ensures that ads always show the correct assets that are active at that time.

Asset databases typically have to be integrated with CDN infrastructure to ensure that assets can be fetched quickly and that there is no latency introduced by the assets being stored in an asset database.

Rule Evaluation and Execution

Personalized advertisements require logic to be coded in them to dictate under what circumstances each version of the creative or dynamic messaging should be rendered. A personalized ad is really a combination of three key elements, as shown in Figure 18.1.

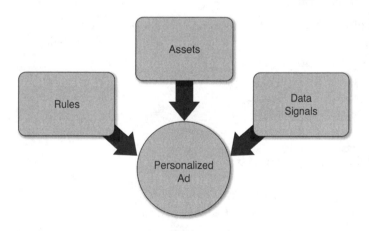

Figure 18.1 Personalized ad execution

Traditionally, while building personalized ads, the logic to determine what variants of creative and messaging should be rendered in an ad were coded individually into each ad. This process becomes incredibly cumbersome, time-consuming, and error prone especially as rules get complex and the rules have to be coded into each variation of the ad. First-generation dynamic ad serving platforms usually did this coding using the Adobe Flash programming language. Unfortunately, in addition to this process being cumbersome and inefficient, Adobe's Flash code, while once a great way to make sure the rules and code worked across browsers, now simply does not work when the ad is rendered on a mobile device because mobile devices do not support the Adobe Flash programming language.

Modern dynamic ad serving technology has solved this problem by abstracting away the rules from the ad. Much like a CMS avoids the need to have all assets physically hard coded into the ad, a dynamic rules engine enables modern ad servers to have these rules set up separately from the ad. Rules get evaluated each time an ad is served, and the rules determine, based on the data signals, which of the assets should be rendered in the ad. Since the rules are evaluated for each ad call and can themselves be pretty complex, it is of course critical that such dynamic rules engines be built to have the ability to process rules within milliseconds.

In addition to making the process of developing such ads much easier and more scalable, this approach also ensures that the logic and code for rule evaluation does not depend on the browser or device it is running on as it is being executed on the ad server's cloud software rather than within the ad itself.

Scalability Considerations

Dynamic advertising campaigns in general tend to be large. In fact, the need to further segment and serve targeted messaging to individuals generally makes sense only for campaigns that seek to deliver to a very large audience.

Personalized ad serving platforms need to be built in such a way that they factor in the very high volumes of impressions—typically in the hundreds of millions to billions of impressions. For each ad impression, data signals need to be retrieved and evaluated, rules need to be executed against the data signals, and assets matching the rule results need to be retrieved and rendered in the ad. All this needs to happen within the few milliseconds available to render an ad on a site or a mobile app.

Internet connections and speed—especially as we spend increasing amounts of our time on data/Wi-Fi networks—are somewhat unreliable, and failures can and will occur when dynamic ad assembly is occurring. The following sections describe the typical failures and remedies for them.

API Response Times and Failure

API failure can occur when either a data signal or an asset service is down. For example, when a call is made to retrieve the latest weather data or geographic data, if the service is down, the API call may fail. If it does, of course the ad should still be rendered—but not with blank weather or blank messaging where the weather-related message should have been. There are a few solutions to this. The first, *service caching*, is available with more advanced dynamic ad serving platforms. With service caching, the dynamic ad server keeps a local copy of the data signal that may not be exactly up to date in real time but will be close enough to still render the ad correctly. For example, weather data can be cached and looked up even if the real-time API call fails.

Sometimes the issue is not that the API is failing but that it is simply taking too long to return results. Here again, advanced dynamic ad serving platforms have time-outs that kick in if an API call is not returning within a preset time, and then the server uses either a default value for the service or does a lookup on the cached data instead.

Asset Latency

Asset latency refers to the fact that assets need to be retrieved dynamically for personalized ads, and so it is very critical to ensure that a dynamic ad serving platform is built in such a way to ensure that such asset retrievals happen well within the expected time for the ad to render correctly.

A CMS that is part of a dynamic ad serving platform enables a very scalable way of ensuring that assets are not hard coded into the ad and also ensures that the ad can load quickly as it will be loading only the assets that will be rendered.

The CMS itself needs to be scalable and needs to ensure that it can deliver assets quickly and reliably on demand. This is often accomplished using a CDN cloud infrastructure. CDNs work by distributing copies of content across a large number of geographically dispersed computers located on reliable networks. These edge servers ensure that when a request is made for a file or an asset (e.g., image, video, animation file, etc.), the asset is delivered from the edge server that is closest to where the user/requester is located. So, for example, even though the physical data center where the original assets are stored may be in New York, a user in Palo Alto, California, will be immediately and quickly served an image asset in a personalized ad because that image is most likely being served from a local copy on an edge server located in or near Palo Alto.

Another factor that affects latency is, of course, the size of the assets. It is important to ensure that assets—especially video files and animations—are kept to smaller sizes so that they load quickly. Even with a CDN, large file sizes can significantly slow down load times for the ad and its components. Video files in particular need to be compressed to ensure minimal latency while loading.

Matching and Rule Execution

Personalized advertisements require the matching of many data signals, several rules, and sometimes thousands of assets. They also involve making a decision about what creative message to deliver. And all this typically happens in less than 100 milliseconds.

The process of matching a data signal or cookie or other index needs to be very efficient. Ad platforms that tried to do this within the ad usually failed pretty badly because as the data set got larger, first it had to be fetched to the browser, which took awhile, and then the match had to be done, using the power only of the browser. Especially on mobile devices, where processor power is minimal, this became problematic, resulting in ads that often did not render.

Rule execution is another area where scale is needed, since rules can get quite complex and execution often involves looking up and processing vast amounts of data—which needs to be done in a few milliseconds in most cases. For some types of data, the data can be preprocessed as much as possible so that the matching process does not require too much computing power, but when working with real-time signals (e.g., weather, geography/IP, etc.), the processing of rules has to be lightning fast.

For the same reasons, platforms that try to perform rule execution within the ad on the client browser often fail because there isn't sufficient computing power to do this within a web browser.

One of the ways to ensure that rule execution is not overly complex is to also preprocess the data signals in such a way that when they are presented to a rule, the rule becomes a simple match rule rather than a very complex rule. This may be critical because the rule has to be evaluated and executed at the time the ad is being served, while the preprocessing of the data can be done ahead of time, thus avoiding all that extra processing overhead.

19

Conversion Tracking and Attribution

Dynamic creative optimization (DCO), an early form of personalized advertising, was used to try to figure out what combinations of creative and messaging produced the best results in converting users to customers. As a result of DCO, many efforts at personalization of ads are also focused on tracking the impact of personalization on conversion (also called attribution).

Attribution itself is a broad subject. For many brands, it involves trying to measure which marketing channels/media are producing the best results in terms of converting prospects to customers. This is often much easier said than done due to the complexities (or impossibility) of identifying a user across media channels like TV, print, and digital—and even within digital, across email, social media, display advertising, etc.

Within the sphere of personalized digital advertising, though, conversion tracking and attribution are critical, especially as there are many dynamic variants of creative and messaging.

When measuring personalized ad performance, it is critical that a few key metrics be measured and reported on:

- **Click-throughs:** This measures when a user clicked through an ad to the brand's landing page. Note that this is a bit more than a user just clicking on an ad. Brands want to know that a click was intentional—that the user actually landed on the page rather than closing the page because she inadvertently clicked on the ad.

- **View-throughs:** This measures whether a user, after seeing an ad, eventually visited the brand's website or landing page, for example, via a Google search. This shows that the advertisement did have an effect on the user, even though she didn't click directly on the ad.

- **Conversions:** This measures whether the user went to the website and actually took some specific action—typically a purchase. Depending on the objective of the campaign, the action may be something else; for example, for a B2B campaign, it may be downloading a white paper, filling out a lead form, etc.

All these metrics that are critical to measuring the effectiveness of a dynamic ad campaign need to be measured and recorded at the level of the creative variant in the ad. In other words, it is critical for a brand to know which particular message or creative combination produced the best conversion metrics. Many dynamic ad platforms, especially the first-generation products, don't have the ability to track and report at the creative variant level because all the tracking and measurement has to be hard-coded into each ad, and it is often too cumbersome and expensive to do so. Even when this is done manually, the process is extremely error prone and often leads to erroneous conclusions.

New dynamic ad serving platforms are able to record these metrics automatically since all the elements of the ad are dynamically served and so any click-throughs or view-throughs are tagged with information about which creative variant was being served when the reporting event occurred. For example, when the user clicks on an ad, the system records not only the click but also the dynamic creative variant that the user saw when he clicked on the ad.

In order to make these metrics work correctly, an additional step is required. Dynamic ad platforms need to have a snippet of code on the brand's website that informs the platform when a user who has seen the ad clicks through, views through, or converts on the site. This is done using a piece of code called a *tracking tag*, which is usually generated by the ad serving platform. A tracking tag, which is usually a piece of JavaScript/HTML code, has to be placed in several locations on the site where conversions may occur.

Until recently, this process was very cumbersome. Recently, however, most sites have implemented *container tags*, which, as their name implies, contain other tags. A site needs to do some work to implement container tags, but once that is done, any tracking tag from any ad server can be uploaded and executed by that container tag, avoiding the need to make changes to the site each time a new campaign is launched. Container tags are available from Adobe, Google, and a few other vendors and are most likely already available on a brand's website.

A tracking tag works by looking up a cookie that was dropped by the ad as soon as it was served to a user. This cookie contains information that the tracking tag can then use to report click-throughs, view-throughs, and conversions.

Attribution in the case of personalized ads is about being able to identify the creative variants that had the best conversion metrics. This kind of attribution tracking is often provided by a dynamic ad serving platform. However, sometimes when attribution tracking is desired across channels (e.g., email, display, etc.), it may be best to use specialized conversion tracking software that works with all the different channels and can take conversion data via an API from the dynamic ad server and record it along with data from other channels so comparisons can be done to determine how each channel performed with respect to conversions.

20

Case Studies

This chapter presents a few case studies of campaigns my company Jivox (which develops technology for personalization of advertisements for major brands) has been involved with. These use cases illustrate the various ways in which dynamic ad personalization can be done. Each example is unique in terms of the data signals used, the complexity of rules and algorithms, and the complexity of managing the dynamic assets and bringing efficiencies and scale to the process through the use of technology.

While these are actual use cases that did run and were viewed by millions of people, I decided not to use the names of the brands themselves. (For more details and examples of these and other ad campaigns, visit www.jivox.com/dynamicads.)

Major Liquor Brand Gets in the Moment

Alcohol is often associated with fun and enjoyment, and alcohol brands are a perfect category for personalized advertising. Drinking can be associated with a wide variety of social activities, so when John White (not the brand's real name) embarked on a personalized and dynamic ad campaign, there was no shortage of ways in which the ads could be personalized and made relevant.

The challenge was instead about picking the relevant data signals that could be used to more effectively personalize the ads.

One of the first challenges, of course, was to figure out who was supposed to figure out what data signals and rules to use to personalize the ads. After much discussion, the conclusion was that it had to be a collaborative effort between the creative team/brand, the media team, and the dynamic ad serving platform provider (my company Jivox).

We first came up with a strawman of data signals to consider and ended up proposing five signals:

- **Weather:** The idea was to reference the weather to find an excuse to have a drink.

- **Sports:** The goal was to identify local sporting events in each city and reference the event in the advertisements to get people to think about John White when they thought of the game. Tailgating was one of the messaging ideas tied to the games.

- **Entertainment:** The goal was to identify entertainment events—such as the Grammys, Oscars, local concerts, etc.— and tie the idea of having a drink to participating in or watching these entertainment events.

- **Twitter trending:** The goal was to identify the top Twitter trends and use them to trigger engagement by speaking to a specific topic that everyone was talking about.

- **Holidays:** The idea here was to tie drinking to holidays—for example, "It's the Fourth of July; fire up the barbecue and have a John White."

These signals were provided to the creative agency, which was to then develop a framework for when the various data signals and rules would cause different messaging to be displayed. The agency needed to set up this framework in our dynamic ad serving platform.

We had developed some worksheets internally to make it easy for the creative team and the brand to create, review, and approve various messaging and visuals for each of the data signals and trigger conditions listed here. These worksheets proved to be invaluable in ensuring that everyone had a clear idea of what users were going to see and experience when the campaign went live. You can see some examples of these worksheets in Appendix A, "Sample Worksheets for Dynamic Ad Campaigns."

Next came the data signal setup. Certain data signals (e.g., weather signals) could be accessed directly via APIs built into the Jivox platform. So the process here only involved configuring the appropriate weather trigger conditions as the data was readily available.

For the sports and entertainment data signals, an extensive database of sporting and local entertainment events was set up in the Jivox dynamic ad platform and indexed with geographic information so that the right sporting and entertainment events could be picked, based on where the user was geographically located. The sporting events included more than 200 NFL games and 150 NCAA games. The local entertainment events numbered about 40 in major cities around the United States.

A holiday database was also set up in the Jivox platform. It contained the major holidays and celebrations in the United States.

Once these databases were set up and indexed, the creative team simply set up messaging for each of them.

Dynamic Creative Setup

Once the data signals, rules, and assets/messaging were decided upon, using the Jivox workflow tools, the dynamic creative could be set up.

Each data signal/rule combination would result in a specific version of the advertisement being rendered. The total number of such variations ended up being more than 3,000 due to the various permutations and combinations of data signals and rules set up.

In order to do this in a scalable fashion, the Jivox platform supports asset groups. An *asset group* is a set of displayable assets (e.g., images, text, animations, video) that should be rendered in an ad when a certain rule evaluates to true.

Once the asset groups were set up, the rules were encoded using the dynamic ad rules user interface (see Figure 20.1). This rules interface enables very simple to very complex rules to be specified, without requiring any code to be written, and it is easy enough for non-programmers to operate.

The user interface also allows for previewing and testing the rules, data signals, and assets to ensure that everything looks and behaves as expected. A preview tool allowed users to see all the dynamic creative variations and approve them before launch.

Figure 20.1 Dynamic ad rules user interface

Once all the previews were approved, the campaign was ready to launch. The entire set of 3,000 dynamic variants of the ad were launched from just 4 ad tags, one each for each of the ad sizes: 300×250, 728×90, 160×600, and 300×600. The campaign was mostly run on a programmatic platform.

Measurement and Optimization

The primary method for determining campaign success was a brand lift study and engagement data from the advertisements themselves. The Jivox platform automatically tagged each of the assets and asset groups so that interaction rates, click-throughs, etc., were recorded in such a way that it was easy to tell which of the creative variants performed the best. The brand lift study offered valuable insights about the impact the campaign had on user awareness of the brand and how the campaign influenced their intent to purchase the product.

Results and the Future

This campaign was a sophisticated example of personalized advertising. The number of data signals used and the number of creative variants resulted in a very customized version of the ad. If you lived in Seattle, for example, and it was a sunny day (a rare event in Seattle), the ad showed a rising sun and had a message that said "Today's forecast: 72 and sunny. Enjoy John White"; if the Seahawks were playing, the advertisement said something like "Blue & green, see you at the tailgate with a John White."

Despite delivering over 3,000 creative variations, the entire setup process was completed in about two weeks, and the campaign delivered detailed metrics that proved invaluable for optimizing the campaign.

For the future of this and other beverage brands, it would be very impactful if sponsored events could be integrated into the personalized advertisements. For example, if the brand were to sponsor a race or sporting event, footage like images, video, and interviews could be made part of the content in the personalized ad.

This campaign did not use any profile data, so that would be a further personalization. It would, for example, have been useful to serve sports-related content to known sports enthusiasts, especially if the profile data was fine-grained enough to show segments of people who liked baseball, football, soccer, etc. This would have allowed the brand to message a specific sport to an individual rather than all sports to everyone.

The success with this campaign has created a great blueprint for the media agency to enable all of its other brands to create similar campaigns using data to drive personalized advertising.

Insurance Agents with a Personal Touch

Insurance companies often operate in a franchise model where agents sell their services. The agents are independent business owners and run their own businesses under license from the insurance company. Along with providing underwriting and other services to each agent, the insurance corporation also provides marketing services.

Each agent is required to co-pay for the marketing services. The agents often have their own websites (sometimes locally branded landing pages within the corporate website), and each would like to build a brand for himself or herself in the local market, much as real estate agents do.

In addition to building the overall brand, the insurance company is also responsible for bringing leads and business to each agent. Because agents pay for a portion of the advertising campaigns, they would like a personalized ad to be shown in the area where they operate so that people who are looking for insurance products know who to go to in order to do so.

Working on a campaign for a national insurance agency to create a dynamic advertising campaign that enabled a personalized view of each agent in the network was a great showcase for how personalized advertising can be delivered at scale with the right technology.

The challenge involved creating a campaign that would have the personal details of more than 1,500 agents delivered in each advertisement so the agents could build a local brand while leveraging the name recognition of the national insurance brand.

Instead of running 1,500 campaigns, the insurance company wanted to run a single campaign personalized to each geography, with the information of the local agent servicing that geography.

In order to do this effectively, the advertisement had to be personalized with the information of the more than 1,500 agents, with photograph, address, phone number, and a click-through to the personalized landing page of each agent.

It was also important for each agent to be able to see that he or she was getting the amount of media paid for (in terms of recorded impressions with the creative) and to track the number of clicks to his or her website.

Clearly, the solution was not to create more than 1,500 ads, test each of them, and make sure they were all encoded correctly, with the correct assets for each agent. The solution they initially tried was to code a template using Adobe Flash and then read the assets and render them in the ad. This sounded easy enough, but the problem was that the images, text, and other assets sent by each of the agents were of different sizes and lengths, and so the ads kept breaking due to the fact that some of the assets could not fit in the template. The ads had problems loading and rendering, too, because the amount of data that had to be processed without a true rules engine to do the matching was requiring that extensive time be spent in the search for the matching assets. To make matters worse, the lack of a robust CMS was causing processing delays in fetching the assets and causing delays in the loading of the ad and its assets.

The use of the Jivox dynamic ad platform resolved all these issues because once a layout was designed with dummy (virtual) assets, all the actual assets were fed in dynamically via an asset database. The dynamic layout capability in the platform was able to resize the assets and have them render correctly each time, and the click-through to each site was also fed in via the asset database dynamically. A virtual click-tracking capability in the layout enabled the click-through URL to be changed each time dynamically, depending on where the ad was being served and what agent's assets and click-through URL needed to be used for the ad.

At runtime, the ads were able to render the assets very rapidly because they were fetched from the dynamic CMS with its own CDN, which ensured minimal latency of assets.

The data signal that was initially used to determine when to serve one agent's creative over another came from the programmatic media buying platform being used to execute the campaign. In the first run of the campaign, each agent's campaign was set up as an individual campaign in the DSP. Therefore, all that had to be done was for the DSP to substitute a macro in the ad tag that provided the dynamic ad platform (Jivox) that the direct index needed to match the assets for each agent. This mapping was done using the Jivox dynamic ads rules user interface.

Results and Future Opportunities

The first attempt at this campaign was done before we got involved, using custom coding of templates. It had a lot of issues, as described above, and it was an expensive and time-consuming process to get the campaign up and running and delivering correctly. Redeploying the campaign via the Jivox dynamic ad personalization platform took only two weeks. The main reason for this was that the platform was designed specifically for this purpose, and it demonstrated the speed and scale to which such campaigns can be delivered, using the right technology platform.

The future opportunities here are to integrate data like purchase data from third parties so that the ads can be customized for specific insurance products that may be relevant to the user seeing the ad. For example, data from auto websites, real estate sites, etc., could be used to predict that the user might be in the market for a new home, and this could be used to customize the ad experience with specific insurance products that might be of more interest than just knowing who the local agent is.

These capabilities apply to other types of insurance, too. Home insurance needs tend to change with each purchase or sale of a home, and a move might be indicative of an upgrade or downgrade of financial status. Switching insurers may be one way people with such changes in financial means adjust their spending. Time is of the essence in getting to these customers, though, since the purchase/sale decision may be happening concurrently with assessing insurance needs, so using home purchase research data in a predictive manner is much more critical than using sales data.

Weather data can also be used to predict when people are more likely thinking about weather insurance products. When it's raining, people tend to worry more about flood insurance.

Insurance ads can also be personalized with local accident and theft statistics. For example, knowing that there have been recent break-ins in an area may prompt users to get insurance for their valuables. Similarly, knowing that the accident rate has increased may prompt a reevaluation of auto insurance for lower deductibles.

Auto purchase data can also be used to personalize and serve insurance ads. For example, the same data signals that are predictive of automobile purchase are also early signals of insurance purchase, so using data from auto sites or DMPs of auto intenders may be a great way to personalize insurance ads to first-time buyers. This is a critical onboarding time for insurance buyers as most second- or third-time auto buyers tend to simply stick with their current insurance provider.

Insurance needs and budgets also change with age. For example, students who have just gotten their first car are often very budget conscious, and so the messaging to them should emphasize price and cost savings. People with families and more established careers tend to look more at coverage and safety and are often somewhat less price conscious. Similarly, this reverses again when people are ready to retire.

Global Hotel Chain Makes It Personal

A global hotel chain was looking to leverage data it had from its global website, where customers often went to search for hotels before they purchased from discount hotel sites or perhaps even a rival chain.

The chain's goal was to gather data from user preferences, deduced from the users' activity on the chain's website. The chain wanted to then use that data to personalize its national ad campaigns.

When a user browsed the brand's main website, she would navigate via search or other means to find hotels in her price range at the location she was planning to visit. This information was then recorded in the user's browser cookie so that it could be referenced in the brand's national advertising programs to personalize the advertisement to that user's individual preferences.

The personalization would go much further than just showing the customer the hotel property she had browsed while on the site; it would also provide real-time special offers that were available for the particular property. The chain hoped that the customer would be enticed by one of the offers to book the hotel room.

In order to set up personalized advertisements for the brand, the ads were designed to have an image of the specific hotel property the customer had browsed on the site. This would provide the customer with a visual reminder that she had earlier expressed interest in the hotel property. The ad would also have a list of special offers available for that particular property.

The data signal in this case was simply a preference selection of the hotel that was recorded in the customer's cookie. Using the Jivox dynamic ad platform's data engine, the cookie was easily read, and its contents were made available to the dynamic rules engine to do the matching against the assets and information for that specific hotel property when the advertisement was served to the customer.

Once the rule was set up to do the matching, the assets for each hotel property were set up as asset databases in the Jivox dynamic ad platform. Each asset group had the image of the hotel property and some information about it, as well as a click-through URL in case the user clicked on the ad. The special offers were delivered to the ad via a dynamic RSS feed, which would enable the special offers to always represent the latest offers made available by the hotel. It would also ensure that older offers that were no longer available would not show in any of the advertisements.

Within each advertisement at runtime, the image, description, and click-through for the hotel property had to be personalized to the customer the ad was being served to. In addition, the special offers feed for that particular property was also displayed in the ad. If the user clicked on any one of the offers, she would be taken to the hotel website, where she could redeem the specific offer.

Results and the Future

In this case, the entire setup of the dynamic images, descriptions, tracking tags for the cookies, and dynamic RSS feeds was done in two weeks. The data signal from the website about the user's hotel preference is just the beginning in terms of personalizing advertisements for the chain's customers. Some of the future possibilities include using third-party profile data to determine the budget range for the traveler and offer up the hotel properties with the matching price bands. Also, now data related to travel patterns of individuals is starting to be available and can be used to serve up offers in the cities the traveler frequents.

Building up this kind of personalization capability will in the future allow the hotel chain to offer upsells of other properties, like vacations and condo rentals attached to their hotel properties. To upsell such products, other data like locations the user frequently travels to, demographics (e.g., family size), net worth estimates, etc., can be very valuable in helping decide what products would be appropriate for such upsell offers.

Upsells within a hotel property could also be an interesting proposition (e.g., a spa treatment, dinner at the restaurant, etc.). Geo location data can confirm that the user is at or near a hotel property and cause a personalized ad to pop up for that user.

Members of the hotel chain's loyalty program could also be offered special incentives and perhaps be prompted to use their accumulated points for amenities at the hotel where they book a stay.

Hotels could also benefit from second-party data, perhaps in exchanges with airlines and car rental companies, to significantly increase their knowledge and data on customers and allow them to even more precisely pinpoint offers and ensure that they are providing exactly what the customer may be in the market for.

How to Follow a Soccer Team

Following a soccer team can be a daunting task. Each game is often an exciting 90 minutes of nonstop action, and the results, as we all saw in World Cup 2014, are utterly unpredictable. So when a soccer team wanted to make ads for its games completely dynamic and personalized, that made perfect sense.

Each ad for the team had to change, depending on which team it was going to play next and where the game was to be played.

The advertisement itself had a skin to match the colors of the team as well as colors of the next opposing team, both teams' logos, and images of the top players on each team.

As the season progressed, a few hours after each game, all assets had to be updated in the live ads.

We had worked with the creative agency on a workflow process so that as soon as the assets were available, they could be swapped into the live campaign. A versioning system in the Jivox dynamic ad platform allowed the brand and creative agency to preview the ads before updating the live campaign. As soon as the brand team approved the previews, a single push of a button published the new assets into the live ad campaign.

The campaign was run in a programmatic environment via a DSP, and for the six-month period during which several games were played, the same ad tags were live, and nothing had to be changed as all the assets and changes happened in the Jivox ad platform's CMS.

Results and the Future

User engagement for this campaign was very high as users marveled at how quickly the ads knew who the team was playing next literally by the time they got home after the game and got in front of their computers.

Campaigns for sporting events have a lot of content produced at the event. This ad campaign could be updated with intermediate results or showcase what will happen next. The ability to purchase tickets and the real-time status of ticket availability in the ad would make it very compelling for procrastinators to buy tickets before they run out.

For sporting series, live footage from the game could also be made available as a stream into the ad campaign. This could be a great way to get new fans hooked on the game. If engagement time is a metric for success of an ad campaign, this will definitely win out over almost anything else!

Sports also tie into many other brands, like alcohol, power drinks, sporting gear, cars, etc. If you ever go up to the Squaw Valley ski resort in California, you will see muscle cars with drinks like Red Bull and Monster, as well as cars and sporting gear tents dotting the landscape as skiers battle each other to get on the lifts. Tie-ins to these other products could be done digitally. Advertisements from Red Bull, Monster, and auto brands could feature real-time content from the ski resorts, targeted using geographic data to the local area from which skiers go skiing. Both brands would benefit: Squaw Valley would get skiers, who would hopefully drink Red Bull while on the slopes.

The ads could of course also broadcast content from various sports and use profile data to showcase content from the user's favorite sport to drive greater engagement.

It's Showtime!

Entertainment brands often struggle with the fact that while they have very large amounts of content that they actually own, the very tight deadlines and late availability of approved assets to use make it very difficult for them to realize the true potential of content in advertising.

We worked with an entertainment brand that was used to having to make manual edits to ad creative code, often with only a few hours available to try to incorporate some new video footage or creative messaging. The issue was that they usually wanted to have different messaging leading up to the show's premiere, new messaging the day of the premiere, and new messaging and assets the day after. The old process of manual edits was very problematic, and swapping out the new messaging was very challenging, even if the edits could be done in time.

One of the key issues was that because multiple ads had to be created for each variation of messaging and assets, ads often said the wrong thing, depending on the viewer's time zone. For example, some messaging was supposed to say "Premieres tonight" on the day of the premiere and "Premieres tomorrow" the day before the premiere. However, between the hours of 9:00 p.m. PST and midnight PST, both were true in different parts of the country.

The problem was that the older technology and process for developing the ads required the entire creative to be swapped: It could say only one message or the other. With the Jivox dynamic ad platform, the ad creative was programmed with the "Schedule data service," which uses the local time zone of the user to calculate the local time and then retrieve the correct set of assets from the platform's CMS, where all versions of the creative—including messaging, video files, and animations—were stored. This allowed the whole team to set everything up and be fast asleep while the platform did the job of dynamically swapping out the messaging and assets for the users who needed the swap.

The dynamic ad platform also allowed easy swaps of assets such as new video footage that became available for the show.

Results and the Future

The campaign ran across many publishers and was one of the largest campaigns ever run by the TV network; it was a great success. The fact that all of the dynamic capabilities also worked across all mobile devices was a first for the brand. (Previous campaigns had shown static fallbacks as Adobe Flash technology was used for development of the ads.)

Dynamic and personalized advertising is relevant to entertainment brands because they produce a lot of content, and the content has a very finite shelf life, so the ability to use content immediately is of great value to entertainment brands.

Entertainment brands are also seeking "tune-ins"—that is, trying to get people to tune in to the network show or head to the theater to watch their shows. Personalization can make that easier, for example, by using geographic data to show local theaters on a map or even perhaps allowing tickets to be purchased from within the ad.

For tune-in, one of the typical challenges is that a TV show appears on different channel numbers on different cable systems, so it has been challenging to direct a user to a particular channel. Now, with personalization technology, data about channel lineups can be used to personalize an ad for each individual, so everyone knows exactly which channel to tune in to for the show. It is also possible now to click on an ad and record a show if the user is logged into the cable network's portal or can enter credentials. Most cable providers are also household Internet service providers and so can allow a user to program a DVR via the web.

Social media plays a big role in entertainment, and so being able to tie in social signals and messaging often creates greater engagement.

While entertainment brands are only now waking up to the idea of dynamic and real-time personalized messaging in their ads, their consumers have already taken matters into their own hands and are using social media to communicate in real time with fans.

During the 2014 World Cup Soccer semifinal game in Brazil, where Germany trounced Brazil, fans generated the most tweets ever recorded for a single event: 35.6 million. Shortly thereafter, the finals in which Germany won against Argentina generated 32.1 million tweets. The interesting thing is that not only were consumers tweeting, they were creating very clever content and publishing it along with their tweets.

Brands need to be in this kind of conversation going on between 35.6 million people—and I don't mean they should run out and buy Twitter ads. I mean all of their media at that moment could have tapped into the conversation by dynamically messaging through media that they were probably already buying and serving ads to.

Tying social media trending topics into entertainment creative is a great way to create engagement by tapping into what people are thinking about. We have produced some entertainment ads where the users can tweet in real time from the ad and have the tweets be sent back out to the ads. I know that marketers are thinking "No way," minds racing through all the things people could say in tweets that they definitely don't want appearing in their ads.

We learned this the hard way with another brand, when they asked to have a live Twitter feed in the brand's ad. It sounded like a great idea until we got a panicked call one day while the campaign was in flight to take down the campaign immediately because someone had just tweeted a racial slur right into the ad. What we learned from this was to implement a real-time approval system in which the marketer has an app to use to approve each tweet to be retweeted to the brand handle that was doing all the tweeting in the ad. This allowed the brand to keep the authenticity of the tweets and yet avoid the PR nightmares of tweets gone wild.

Weather data also can play a key role in marketing TV programming. Messaging things like "It's snowing outside; time for a dose of *Modern Family*" could drive greater viewership. We don't often think about it consciously, but I bet we could do an analysis of our movie- watching habits and realize that we are influenced by weather and probably a few other things that trigger us to watch a TV show or movie.

The Right Car for You

Buying a car is a very personal decision. If you interviewed five people and asked why they bought exactly the same car, they would give you five different answers. The answers might be: "It's a very powerful car," "It looks really cool," "It has a lot of trunk space," "I feel very safe driving it," and "I got a good deal on it." So personalization is clearly a great opportunity for automobile advertisers.

We worked with a premium auto brand to deliver five different tag lines to different audience segments within the brand's target consumer base. The brand was targeting millennials, who are very independent in thinking and are heavy users of social media and mobile devices.

The brand recognized the various reasons people buy cars and crafted messages that would be contextually relevant, based on the site the ad was being served on. For example, ads served on CNNMoney.com spoke to the aspirational aspects of the car: growing up, success, and leadership. On publishers like Wired.com and Car and Driver, the ads spoke to the supercar-like performance of the car. On sites like Esquire.com and Glamour, the ads spoke to the "sex appeal" of the car.

This was also one of the first ads to showcase an Instagram feed of images from users of the car—another great way to use dynamic content to engage users visually and emotionally.

Results and the Future

The campaign was incredibly successful for the brand and was hailed by the trade press as one of the most successful auto campaigns ever. The campaign had to be halted as the brand ran out of inventory, and for the first time in the brand's history, sales surpassed those of the competition.

This was one of the earliest campaigns where true dynamic features were used by a major auto brand. At that time, the technology available was limited, so it was quite remarkable to be able to execute the campaign flawlessly.

The auto category lends itself very well to personalization, and these are a few things auto campaigns can and should consider as personalization options:

- **Auto site-based personalization:** Most auto sites have very extensive product information and personalization data. Customers come to the site to browse products, where they indicate their preference of the type of car. They also often select colors, specific features, etc., of the car. All this is very valuable information that can be tapped to personalize advertising to an individual.

- **Demographic and profile data:** Purchasing an automobile is a decision that different individuals make using entirely different criteria. Men and women pick cars using different mindsets. Age plays a role in selection, too. Even for the same car model, gender and age may play a role in selection. For example, while picking an SUV, women may pay more attention to cargo space, floor mats, and safety features, while men may pay more attention to the sound system, engine specs, and electronics. This is not to say that they each don't care about the other features, just that a person's role in a family often causes him or her to look at things differently.

- **Weather:** Weather is an important data signal that can be used very effectively to personalize auto ads. If you live in California, on a warm day, you might picture a car being handy to take to the beach. On a cold day, you might be thinking about skiing. Changing the skins and other animations in an ad based on weather can have a great impact on the emotional tie-in, which often leads to purchase.

- **Geography:** Despite the success of online buying from eBay motors and other sites, most buyers want to see and test drive a car before making a purchase. Knowing where the nearest dealer is or even getting a reminder that the nearest dealer is on the way to the grocery store may be the prompt needed to get someone to go visit the dealer. Ads can be personalized to show a map of where the nearest dealer is, using the user's IP address or GPS coordinates.

- **Behavioral data:** Auto purchasers tend to do a lot of research before they buy. They often visit several sites, like Car and Driver to read reviews, Kelley Blue Book's KBB.com to check on trade-in values, brand sites to check out features, etc. All these are buying signals. Most DMPs provide audience segments of "auto intenders," and this data is invaluable in personalizing a message to the individual. Often it is even possible to do this based on the stage of "purchase funnel" the user may be in. For example, if someone is simply researching features, he may be in earlier stages of purchase consideration, but if he is on KBB.com, he may be getting close to a purchase decision.

Auto brands can definitely benefit very significantly from personalization of their advertising. Auto brands were some of the earliest brands to embrace dynamic creative optimization. Due to the very large amounts of advertising they do, they needed ways to somehow lift performance and measure as much as possible to figure out what resonates. This unfortunately is still a bit backward looking and puts too much focus on trying to see what is working in terms of dynamic creative instead of really starting with data and information and working toward the messaging that ought to be delivered, based on knowledge of the consumer.

Telcos Offer Choice

Cable companies and satellite providers, in an attempt to fend off competition from video-on-demand services like Netflix and Amazon, are finally starting to unbundle products rather than force programming down a customer's throat for a fat monthly fee that is justified by the offer of "hundreds of channels." Telcos must now market individual products or sub-bundles, and so personalization and data are becoming very important from a marketing perspective.

Telcos in some ways have a significant advantage over other industries in that they have lots of data about their users. However, they are also the most regulated and scrutinized of all industries as they tend to enjoy monopolies in their regions (except, of course, for satellite TV providers). They therefore have to be very careful about how they use the data they collect.

We worked with a telco to market its bundles. The primary source of data was user activity on the telco's website. Tracking tags on the website were placed to detect which products the user had browsed so that advertisements the person might see on other sites would reflect the packages she had browsed on the telco provider's website.

We were able to handle a number of challenges that the telco had faced with previous attempts at personalization:

- **Difficulty updating creative changes:** As described elsewhere in this book, traditional rich media platforms were built as coding environments, which required Flash programmers to be involved whenever creative changes had to be made. In addition to the creative changes, this triggered an enormous cycle of testing and approvals that made it impossible to turn things around quickly and launch. With the Jivox dynamic ad platform, asset refreshes were simply updated in the CMS or in the asset feed and were immediately available in the live campaign, thus eliminating the long lead times and costs associated with such updates.

- **Failed reporting:** One of the key objectives of the campaign was to track conversions from each of the creative variations. This was very problematic because the platform being used was not capable of dynamically passing creative variant information back to the reporting system. This meant that the ads had to be hard-coded with tracking codes, which often resulted in mistakes and incorrect data being reported back to the attribution and conversion tracking system.

- **Problems with mobile devices:** On mobile devices, the personalization did not work for two reasons. First, the creative was coded in Flash and so would not render on mobile devices. Second, the lack of or difficulties with placing and reading cookies on mobile devices caused conversions—especially those that occurred across screens—not to be recorded correctly. The solution for this was to use Jivox's cross-screen virtual cookie technology to bridge the user activity across devices.

Results and the Future

Telcos are increasingly become more like multi-brand retailers in that they have to carry a variety of products and offer them up via personalized ads so that relevant users are delivered the right messaging about products they are likely to purchase.

Here are a few opportunities for personalization for telco advertising:

- **Conquest advertising:** Most telcos have data on IP address ownership by competing telcos. For example, Comcast would know what IP addresses AT&T owns. This information could be used to customize offers in the ad with specific pricing packages to entice users to switch.

- **Profile-based personalization:** Personalization using only website data has a significant disadvantage in that it doesn't include any data on users who have not come to the website. For example, not every NFL fan would go to DIRECTV's website to browse sports packages. Third-party or second-party data from partners could signal whether someone is a football fan or not, and so the NFL packages could be offered to such users. Still other users might be soccer fans, and for them, the soccer packages could be shown instead.

- **Geo and language personalization:** To attract different ethnic communities to buy language packages, website data alone does not work because many of these folks do not go to the telco's website. Instead, using geographic and language demographics data, ads can be personalized to show specific language packages (e.g., Hispanic, Hindi, etc.) to concentrations of populations in particular geographies.

In the telco world, cable companies face the least competition as they are regulated and are monopolies (at least the cable part of their business). Satellite companies also don't have much competition, given how much capital investment is required to start a satellite company. Phone carriers, especially wireless carriers, face the most intense competition. All of them now are having to compete once again, thanks to the Internet, for services for which they do not hold monopolies (e.g., broadband access, media services, etc.). Not a day goes by without some telco crying foul for some other telco gaining some advantage using legislation and lobbying to its advantage.

Sales of mobile phones by wireless carriers are one of the most intensely competitive areas. These companies are constantly pushing out introductory pricing, special offers, rebates, etc., almost on a daily basis. The head of production at a major agency told me that he would get a call from one of his clients at a large wireless carrier, saying that the competitor had just introduced a special promotion on iPhone plans and that the client wanted all its ads changed IMMEDIATELY to a new offer to counter that one. He lamented that when the client said *immediately*, he meant *immediately*.

What happened next is a good reminder of why dynamic personalized advertising technology is critical for the future of real-time changes in marketing messages. When the client told the head of production at that major agency to change the ads immediately, he had to get several Flash developers on the phone (he actually had to wake many of them up) and have them work overnight, editing and changing every one of the several hundred banner ads that were live. Then everything had to go through QA and go live before the next morning. It was an impossible task. With the upset client calling every few hours, they slowly plodded through editing each one of the hundreds of banner files and got the new messaging live only several days later.

In such businesses, the old idea of planning a big campaign and going through all the media planning (with lots of Excel spreadsheets exchanged) and creative ideation, editing, and approval cycles is clearly not working. That cycle now needs to be completed in hours rather than months. Previously, the technology did not exist either on the media buying side or on the creative side, but now we have both and have an incredible opportunity to transform how we market.

21

Privacy

One of the biggest criticisms of early attempts at personalized advertising has been the *creep factor*, which many describe as the ad that "follows you," with an intimate knowledge of what you have done or what you have browsed online. This has always been a challenging aspect of technologies and methods that attempt to use information to create a better experience for consumers.

A recent incident illustrating this involved the much-beloved and sometimes-reviled cab-hailing service Uber. An executive of Uber was supposed to meet a reporter for an interview. As soon as she walked into Uber's offices, she immediately saw the executive come down the stairs as if he knew the precise moment when she would arrive. Actually, he did. As he very proudly—but perhaps lacking good judgment—told her, he had been tracking her, using a version of the Uber software called God View that uses the same location information that users find so beneficial to hail a cab.

In this case, technology that makes it very easy and efficient to hail a cab simply by using the user's location was being used very inappropriately to track, of all things, a reporter. Imagine how frustrating the Uber app would be to use if in order to hail a cab, you had to call the driver nearest to you and tell him where you were instead of allowing the app to detect and use that information to direct the driver to you. I am sure almost everyone who uses Uber would agree that use of what most of us would consider private information (i.e., our physical location at any time) to personalize an experience for us is very acceptable, provided that Uber does not use that information inappropriately to do something like track a reporter.

There are several instances every day when we share information about ourselves in order to have a service personalize itself to our needs. We as a society are becoming more and more comfortable with it—to the point where Pandora automatically posts the song you are listening to on Facebook—and we think it is cool and not an invasion of our privacy. Pandora, after all, also uses this information to create personalized songs for us to listen to and makes it much easier to listen to songs we like.

Fitness bands, which are all the craze now, are also collecting a lot of personal information—from when someone goes to sleep, to when he or she wakes up, to how much the person walks, to how much the person eats—and provide an analysis of the person's health on a daily basis.

In all these examples, what seems apparent is the notion of "fair trade": That is, as consumers, we are all okay providing our personal information and even having it be used to provide a better service or product to us, as long as there is a fair trade.

If an app company that had location information about us created a paid service where people could pay to know where we are and have been, we would be outraged because we don't consider that fair trade. In fact, that would be an illegal use of information that we shared only because we generally understood that the brand would use the information on a "fair basis" to provide a better product or service to us.

Brands have a tremendous responsibility here, and indeed they have an opportunity to provide vastly more engaging and useful advertising products while safeguarding personal information.

The advertising industry has largely been able to self-regulate itself to ensure that personally identifiable information is not disclosed in the process of targeting advertising or customizing ad experiences. In working with various data providers, it is very clear that all of them follow this ethos very diligently and implement all exchanges or provisioning of data using anonymous handles.

When a personalized advertising platform like Jivox uses a data service, it simply doesn't receive any personally identifiable information from any data source, even if it were available.

The mechanism by which data providers and data services are able to provide very precise information without revealing personally identifiable information is called a *cookie sync* (described in more detail in Chapter 16, "Developing Big Data for Personalization"). In simple terms, this is how the mechanism works: If Service A knows fact X about an individual and wants to provide that information to Service B in return for fact Y that Service B knows about the individual, it performs a cookie sync. When Service A encounters an individual M, it makes a call to Service B (usually via a URL) to say "I just met M, here is my identifier for M." Service B in turn either knows about M from a previous exchange or doesn't, and if it doesn't, it simply responds to Service A with its own identifier for M—say, M1. After this exchange, it is now established between these two services that M and M1 are the same individual, and so any information Service A has or gathers about M can now be passed to Service B and vice versa, using the simple mapping of M to M1.

This exchange ensures that any personally identifiable information about M is never passed between the services. However, preference data, or data that could allow each service to learn more about the user to improve the user's experience, can be exchanged.

The Network Advertising Initiative (NAI) was founded in 2000 as an industry self-regulatory body. It was formed to ensure that its members are able to honor opt outs by consumers who do not want to be targeted with advertising using their online behavioral data. Consumers can go to the NAI website (http://www.network advertising.org) to see a list of member companies that will honor such opt outs and can selectively or collectively opt out of such tracking and targeting.

There have been attempts by browser manufacturers (i.e., Microsoft) to try to implement "do not track" features. However, such attempts have been largely unsuccessful.

Consumers understand that most of the free content and services—like email, maps, and thousands of free apps—are all paid for either directly or indirectly by advertising. Consumers do, however, hate interruptive and irrelevant ads, and when consumers express their distaste for advertising, it is usually directed at ads that simply blast them with irrelevant information about products they will never buy and that increasingly get in the way of their enjoying content on the site.

These attempts to become even more interruptive and lately even blur the line between site content and advertising using so-called native advertising showcase an incredible amount of disregard and disrespect for consumers and an unwillingness by the offending brands and media companies to put in a little extra effort to make ads perform by just simply making them more relevant and engaging.

Brands that understand this and invest in personalization of advertising and marketing will flourish and get significant ROI on their marketing dollars. Consumers who increasingly have more and more power to ignore a brand and influence their friends and other consumers negatively about brands will increasingly shun brands that don't understand this.

22

The Future

One thing is for certain about the future of personalized advertising: Marketers will have more and more data with which to make personalization decisions.

Just in the past few years, an enormous number of new wearable products have been introduced. Mobile phones and tablets created an explosion of data that can be used to personalize advertising. Now wearable devices are generating even more data that is even more personal. For example, wearable exercise and sleep monitors record your sleep patterns, exercise patterns, and, for the zealous who enter the food they eat to track calories, they record food habits. Many electronics manufacturers have introduced watches that are tied to your mobile phone and also measure and inform you of sleep and other personal data.

The "Internet of things" movement to connect every possible electronic device (e.g., dishwashers, microwaves, cars, etc.) means all these devices now are generating and reporting very valuable data to their manufacturers, which in turn can use the data for personalizing and targeting advertisements or can offer that data up to other brands to utilize for marketing.

As customer sensitivity to personal data seems to be declining significantly, marketers are able to push the boundaries even more in personalizing advertising, using even more fine-grained data.

Mobile application developers and media companies have come to the realization that advertising is not the only way to monetize their applications or media. Data has become just as important a currency as advertising. A media publisher that today makes most of its revenue from advertisements placed in its media can now additionally make money by offering its data to marketing platforms or data aggregators.

This creates an explosion of data and significantly lowers prices as data very quickly becomes a commodity. This is a big boon to marketers because they can now make their advertising much more effective, without necessarily spending significantly more on media.

The big challenge with all this data, of course, is that raw data by itself is not very useful for personalizing advertisements or marketing in general. So a big part of the value in the personalization ecosystem is going to be technology and platforms that can aggregate, organize, and make this data available for marketers to use. This is one of the significant challenges with using data for personalization today.

In the past, because data was mostly looked at as historically significant rather than predictive, most data practitioners tended to be more backward looking than forward looking about how to use data. For marketing and personalization, it is critical that data be used in more of a forward-looking manner—that is, in a more predictive manner—than in looking back.

Data practitioners need to learn how to leverage data for predictive use in marketing rather than simply churn out reports that tell marketers what happened. Instead, data practitioners should equip marketers with data that will help them be more proactive in predicting buying patterns and targeting the right messaging to help drive purchase decisions. We will see some very powerful recommendation and predictive technology emerge that will make all the data valuable to marketers.

Data today also has a time value. Our mobile devices have made us able to make decisions on the spot. Before mobile devices, the best we could do was browse the Internet at home, get in our car, go to the mall, and shop around. Today we are browsing and shopping online while waiting in line at a grocery store or waiting for our dentist. Impulse buying and shopping have become the norm. We get updates from our friends via social media that prompt us to buy, and we get text messages from friends wanting to go to the mall.

The ability to process data and use it in real time to market to customers will be imperative for brands to survive in the midst of all this noise and interruption. Yet consumers will not put up with barrages of meaningless emails, special offers, banner ads, etc., and will unsubscribe, block, or do whatever they can to prevent marketers from continuing this barrage. Winning brands will apply data and all the intelligence it brings in a timely fashion and in a moment when a decision is being made to purchase.

The value of data relative to time is also something that will enable brands to recognize at what stage of purchase the user is in. Here again, the intelligent use of data to serve up the right content, information, and messaging will make the difference between a user engaging or ignoring the brand.

Time of the Day

As kinds of data go, time is the easiest and least private data there is. It often doesn't get the respect it should from marketers, and yet our needs throughout a day, week, or month are very time based. We think of breakfast at 7:00 a.m., we think of transportation at 8:00, lunch at noon, a drink at 5:00, and dinner at 7:00. We think of leisure as the weekend approaches, gifts as the holidays approach, movies as the evenings approach, and sleep as the night gets late.... You get the idea.

Why, then, is time not used much in personalized advertising? The entertainment industry perhaps stands out the best in using time (e.g., to deliver customized tune-in messaging). It has messages leading up to an event, the day before the event, the day of the event, and the days after the event.

Liquor brands should think of happy hour and tailgating. Cosmetic brands should be up and about while customers do a quick login before breakfast. Sports brands should message weekend activities as the weekend approaches.

Time needs to be local. We can't be talking about happy hour at the same hour across the country; we have to dynamically message it at a different time in each time zone.

Location: Beacon Technology and Applications

Lately there has been a lot of buzz about beacon technology. *Beacons* are inexpensive transmitters that can be placed at various locations in a store or mall or airport that transmit their location and other basic information using a simple signal delivered via Bluetooth. Most phones are Bluetooth equipped, and applications on such a phone can intercept this signal and figure out where the user is in order to offer up special coupons or other notifications.

Beacon technology has gained a lot of momentum recently due to the fact that there is now a standard for transmitting and receiving beacon signals. This standard, called the iBeacon standard, will likely cause the very rapid proliferation of beacons since a large number of phones can now receive and process such signals.

Mobile phones have GPS devices that can help determine a user's location, and a user's location can also generally (but not necessarily accurately) be determined based on IP address. The missing piece is information on what the location means—and that is what a beacon provides (i.e., context to the location). This context is very valuable to personalization because it allows an even finer grain of personalization to be applied to advertisements since it is now possible to know exactly which aisle of a supermarket a user is strolling.

Large establishments like airports and malls can provide such "personalized ad inventory" to marketers, and marketers in turn can create in-the-moment shopping and purchase triggers.

Hotel chains are experimenting with beacon technology to see if they can deliver special personalized offers while the guest is in the lobby or walking to the spa. Just blasting incessant "buy now" offers will cause consumers to shut down and tune out the brand, but intelligent application of data (e.g., loyalty data, location data, historical purchase data) can be used to make a brand look smart and eager to deliver a very personalized service that even the best concierge may not be able to do.

Privacy

We spoke about privacy earlier. It is very important for us as an industry to manage and self-regulate on privacy because one of the big risks related to the use of data for personalized marketing is consumer backlash at brands abusing their data. Brands and media companies need to carefully preserve user identities and stick purely to the principle of "personalization" rather than "targeting."

Trigger-Based Media Activation and Optimization

A lot of the discussion of personalization has centered around ads themselves. However, there are also opportunities to use data signals to optimize media. Optimization of media can be done in two primary ways. First, media buys can be activated by dynamic trigger conditions, and second, media buys can be optimized based on performance data from personalized ads.

Triggering media buys based on data signals is possible in a programmatic buying environment because each ad impression is purchased on a bid basis (i.e., a bid can be placed only when certain trigger conditions are met on the buying side). Traditionally, programmatic platforms have operated on data signals from the selling side, not the buying side. For example, a publisher could set flags in its inventory to indicate the quality of inventory or even data profiles of the user in the response; if the buyer had requested that particular attribute, he or she could execute the buy. Triggering a media buy from the buying side using data signals puts the controls in the buyers' hands and so can be very powerful because it can be event based. Examples are executing buys for an allergy drug only when the pollen counts are high or buying media during a storm for rain-related products. Similarly, weather triggers can be used to promote cold or warm drinks, executing media buys only when extreme conditions are present. In these cases, the dynamic ad platform would feed in the trigger conditions under which the media transaction should be executed.

Back to Media Upfronts Again?

Personalized advertising enables brands to stop thinking in terms of campaigns with a finite start and end and instead think about continuous conversations with customers and prospects. This changes the advertising process, from being a campaign-by-campaign model to a much more dynamic process, in which there is always a campaign running. By using a dynamic ad personalization platform, brands can control and publish creative and messaging updates to a campaign.

Personalized advertising also changes how media is bought as it makes it easier to execute media buys as upfronts from large publishers with the associated cost savings, knowing that the evergreen media buy can be used to push out messaging and creative that match the brand's sales objectives.

Social Media Platforms Lead the Way

Social media platforms like Facebook and Twitter have been the most progressive in showing the marketing world how data can be a very significant asset in getting the right message to the right person at the right time. Social media has also turned the whole model of media planning, creative, launches, etc., on its head, and brands are increasingly able to push out messaging to consumers when they see an opportunity; they can do so in a matter of hours or days instead of the traditional cycle of weeks or months with display advertising campaigns.

What social media platforms lack is the real estate to offer more compelling ad formats. While Facebook and Twitter continue to introduce bigger ad formats, they have been very cautious about not overwhelming users with large-format ads and losing the very asset they are relying on to attract advertising dollars.

Facebook and Twitter, along with many other publishers, are now starting to offer "audience networks" outside their properties, where they have a bit more leeway and don't run the risk of losing users by bombarding them with advertisements.

These audience networks will start offering very powerful targeting and personalization options for brands, using the tremendous wealth of data that social networks have on users.

Apps, Apps, and More Data

I am starting to believe that data may be an even bigger product for app developers to monetize than ad inventory. Many apps don't lend themselves well to advertising and yet have tremendous amounts of data that are very valuable to marketers. The company Flurry, recently acquired by Yahoo, has amassed data about 540,000 mobile apps and 1.4 billion devices. This gives Flurry a wealth of data to personalize advertising with. And other companies are doing the same thing.

DMPs, DSPs, and data aggregators all are now able to arm marketers with significant amounts of very fine-grained data to deliver precise targeting and personalization.

Much as social networks have discovered the value of data as currency, app developers are starting to see their data as perhaps even more valuable than their inventory. Likewise, I fully expect wearable device developers and all other devices, apps, sites, etc., to start offering their data to marketers.

It seems that the race to make more and more data available will soon create a massive commoditization of data, to a point where it will be less about whether you have data about your customers than about what you are actually doing with it. In fact, we may indeed end up with an embarrassment of riches related to data: We may not know what to do with all of it. Brands have always had a lot of data about their customers. It may not have been real-time data or even as fine grained and varied as what we have now, but marketers have not really used all that data in the past.

The new imperative and excitement—and dare I say hype—about Big Data may be what it takes to get marketers to finally see the value in using data to personalize user engagement and experiences. While we do that, let's not forget: It's not about the data but about how you use it effectively to market. The platforms that can help us harness all this data and turn it into strategic weapons for marketers will be handsomely rewarded.

Minority Report Almost Here?

Personalized advertising today is getting closer to the talking billboards in *Minority Report* as we harness the power of beacons for location-based messaging and identification, data for personalization, and many more screens. It is not hard to see a talking billboard in our future. At the Consumer Electronics Show (CES) in 2015, as I was strolling along, a robot pulled alongside me and started chatting me up. The operator of the robot was in the Ukraine, while the robot was with me in Las Vegas. She was able to see and chat with me, and I ended up taking a picture with her.

If you've seen *Minority Report*, do you remember the even more interesting and sinister piece of technology: the precogs, which were half human and half machine and could predict the future? The idea was that the precogs would let the police know when a crime was about to be committed so they could show up and arrest the person before any damage was done. Every marketer would love to have this kind of technology that can predict when a consumer is about to buy, giving the marketer the ability to message the consumer at that precise moment. Until that happens, we will all have to do with talking billboards and stalking robots.

23

Industry Perspectives

I was inspired to write this book by conversations with some key people in the media and advertising world who all seemed to have a common vision that advertising needs to change and become much more relevant, engaging, and in the moment. They all felt, as I always have, that the industry has largely been repeating the model of "throw a lot out there and see what sticks," even for digital advertising, where we actually can render precisely crafted and targeted messaging on a one-to-one basis to create a dialogue with consumers.

Yes, sophisticated technology was needed to make it all happen, but more importantly, a change in mind-set and attitude among marketers, agencies, and media companies was needed, as was a commitment to making advertising engaging, relevant, and exciting again. Many industries and daily activities we engage in have been made better using technology: Hailing cabs, listening to music, buying books, and keeping in touch with friends have all been transformed and made significantly more efficient. At first, all these innovations were treated as "disruptions" and were resisted until folks in the industry figured out that they could still make money and deliver a service (perhaps a much better one)—a lot more efficiently.

I have enjoyed getting to know these folks and building partnerships with them. We hope together to transform the world of digital advertising into one that is personal, engaging, and exciting again. We want to put the consumer at an equal, respected level with the brand and maybe even let consumers tell us how to market and sell to them.

Without a doubt, these are the key visionaries who are helping transform advertising into something that is relevant, engaging, and— heck yes—even likable.

Gregg Colvin, Chief Operating Officer, Universal McCann USA, an IPG Mediabrands Agency

Background

The average American consumes about 81 hours of media per week and 1,200 ads per day. With such a crowded media landscape, it is next to impossible to win based on share of voice alone. Instead, we need to think beyond impressions and frequency to capturing consumer attention. Put simply, marketers need to own a moment with a message that matters to consumers.

New Data

Personal applications and wearable technology help address this issue by heralding a new era for marketing and data. While traditional analytic sources merely provided a snapshot of an amorphous consumer and his or her media habits writ large, today's personal data is enabling brands to connect with consumers in more profound and immediate ways.

New Platforms

Among the most compelling innovations is the rise of trigger-based advertising platforms. At Universal McCann, we call this *moments marketing*, and tools like ours and the ones developed by AOL and Jivox enable marketers to create personal messaging in real time.

While the technology is sophisticated, the process is simple: We identify relevant moments in media and culture, and we create personalized interactions in order to own moments. In this way, we can leverage a trend for product promotion, leverage an event to create brand loyalty, and leverage any moment to ensure brand relevance. Essentially, we are making daily moments actionable and targeting consumers contextually across devices.

Examples

One of the first cases of using moments marketing involved a popular over-the-counter allergy medicine. The result was simple in its eloquence: Pair insight with real-time events to create a personalized and effective message. In this situation, we knew that users are more likely to purchase the medication when symptoms occur. Using pollen count as the trigger for media, we built scenarios that targeted frequent users with timely forecasting and personalized messaging. Essentially, we optimized media for those consumers at those moments.

Likewise, we worked with Jivox to capture moments of celebration in sports with the Jack Daniels brand. From a planning perspective, we understood that consumers of Jack Daniels were more likely to consume the beverage to celebrate a team win. We identified those teams, and when scores and alerts were announced, we were able to capitalize on the goodwill.

With the proliferation of data and a platform to reach consumers immediately, marketers are constrained only by their creativity. We can utilize stock market indices to deliver real-time media to investors and weather reports to drive sales of skin care lotion. Consider an oil company. Would it rather market to a general audience at home watching television or target media to a driver in rush hour, alongside stories of declining oil and gas prices? It is exponentially more valuable to market in moments of relevance than to plan for general audiences.

Success

The impact of real-time personalized advertising has been exceptional: Brand favorability increases by 49%; consumers are 44% more likely to recommend a brand; and perhaps most importantly, consumers are 37% more likely to purchase the brand. A new planning and buying process can tap into real-time triggers and cultural moments. Simply put: Real time works!

Transformation

All this data and technology have proven transformative in terms of targeting and frequency. We can move away from planning for demographic groups and instead target individuals and move toward planning for moments rather than frequency. I call this seismic shift targeting *people not populations.*

Karin Timpone, Global Marketing Officer, Marriott Worldwide

Today's marketing tools are constantly evolving, and it can often feel like a big task to keep current on the latest technology, promising more and better results. While personalized marketing messaging sounds like a digital affair, I find that many marketing innovations are really invitations to look across the marketing mix using a comprehensive, omni-channel lens.

I believe that keeping an eye on the essential, core objective helps better to direct the outcome. Over the years that I have worked in global marketing, I have been an advocate for the customer and the consumer. This orientation informs my core objective, so I can work across various disciplines to deliver plans that connect marketing strategy with tactics. While connecting the dots takes some think-and-plan time, the main work comes in building a team that takes action, refines it, and can do it again and again. I've used this recipe for success in building never-did-that-before marketing in various industries, spanning consumer goods, technology, entertainment and digital media, travel, and more.

Consider the following tips for your next audacious, personalized marketing endeavor.

Develop Good Definition and Understanding of Your Target Market

Be specific about the target audience that will pay business dividends. Use quantitative analysis as well as qualitative insights on who they are and what they need. Make sure your four *Ps*—product, promotion, price, and place (distribution)—are aligned to meet the target market need. And then make sure your colleagues have a good shorthand definition they can easily repeat. You may be pleasantly surprised how much this can help guide smaller actions that add up to bigger impact.

Personalized marketing upside: Your message will resonate because it will be inherently focused.

Bring Together the Artists and the Scientists

Now more than ever before, marketing is an amalgam of both art and science. Sometimes, though, the organizational design or even a seating plan may not make for organic integration. If your marketing team's skills are siloed into departments where the creative don't sit with the analytics team or the engineers, the key is to bring the right collaborators together. And if you are a marketer with hybrid skills that can write great copy as well as mine data, reach out to another group that can amplify your efforts. Maybe that is an internal operations team or possibly an external marketing partner, agency, or new platform.

Personalized marketing upside: You will increase your potential of the "right message, right person, right time" when good creative chops mix with good targeting acumen.

Test and Learn, Making Bets as You Go

Especially with new marketing technologies, data can help embolden a good plan or redirect a less successful one. A series of tests can provide feedback loops that can provide valuable input on your longer-term strategy. Recently, my team tested a never-did-that-before marketing initiative that was successful, and at the same time we discovered an adjacent use in the operations realm. Another test aimed at audience acquisition found a new benefit for retention. Both illustrate the importance of learning where new data transforms into understanding.

Personalized marketing upside: Testing makes your marketing more like an ongoing, relevant conversation with your customer and consumer.

Ask Your Marketing Partners if They Have Similar Goals

Letting your marketing partners know about your core objective can open a discussion about ways to enhance efforts. In my experience, I've been able to combine resources with marketing partners that are aiming for similar goals. Once again, this may require some effort to connect the dots, but the opportunity to expand your reach is likely worth it.

Personalized marketing upside: Good partnerships with mutual goals can multiply your results.

Consider the Overall Customer Experience

What can the folks on the frontlines contribute as input for your marketing initiatives? These can be guest-facing associates, social media practitioners, or customer care reps who serve to extend the brand experience. If there are new trends or challenges emerging, they can provide a valuable signal.

Personalized marketing upside: Enlist the shadow army of marketers that are around you, especially those closest to your customer. They play an important part in personalizing on another dimension.

Make the Readout Easy

No one needs another dense, difficult report in the inbox. Everyone wants synthesis. Provide a summary that immediately conveys the upshot and a clear path ahead. Do everyone a favor and plan to make your reports timely and portable enough to be cut and pasted into other presentations and proposals. Heck, make 'em fun.

Personalized marketing upside: It's simple—easier collaboration happens when the success metrics are clear.

Peter Minnium, Head Brand Initiatives, Interactive Advertising Bureau (IAB)

As an advertising industry veteran with the gray hair to prove it, I find myself from time to time discussing the industry with other long-time pros. The other day, an acquaintance who leads one of the largest U.S. agencies was reminiscing with a group about when he first started in the business—not quite Mad Men days, but the late 1980s. Afterward, a digital advertising industry friend who was with us commented on how sad it was that our colleague "wished it was still the good ol' days."

I shocked her by saying, "Who doesn't!?" After all, before the explosion of digital advertising, we lived in a linear media world where marketers and publishers were in control, leading consumers as effectively as the Pied Piper with his magic pipe. That was the pinnacle of analog advertising, a time in which professionals practiced a perfected craft and were richly rewarded for it.

Then, the world changed.

Today, digital media and advertising have enabled a level of interaction and dialogue between marketers and consumers whereby the two are becoming equal partners in the advertising experience, often co-creating the meaning of a brand. In this world, marketers are absolutely not in control and, in many cases, are not only not in the lead but are actively following behind the consumer.

As a result, advertising professionals, like my aforementioned friend, must start all over again, learning a new set of rules and tools to achieve the same ends.

Although never of this magnitude, this sort of transition is not entirely new. Advertising in every new medium begins as an awkward accompaniment and, over time, matures and takes on a more natural form, fitting more comfortably within the content. Early television commercials featured nattily dressed radio announcers reading copy to the camera. It took many years for television advertising to find its natural form of mini 30-second stories within the broader program stories. Similarly, early magazine ads were stacked at the back of the book and only became integrated between stories and reflective of the publications' look and feel over time.

The digital banners in the ubiquitous leaderboard and right rail placements that dominated the web for its first 18 years are the equivalent of TV's and magazine's pre-adolescent forms. Too often, these have been out of the reader's activity stream, not mindful of the page content or style, they have not offered the user the ability to interact in the same manner as content on the other parts of the page, and, most damningly for digital, they have failed to tailor the message to the reader.

The good news is that digital advertising is ready to exit its adolescent growth phase. Marketers' ability to create distinct commercial options and brand messages—and agencies' ability to create matching assets—is finally catching up with ad tech's ability to target, render, and serve dynamic creative. The industry is finally beginning to realize its potential to deliver the long-promised but rarely achieved "right ad to the right person at the right time"—in other words, personalized digital advertising.

And that's worth giving up "the good ol' days" for.

Gowthaman Ragothaman, Chief Operating Officer, Mindshare Asia Pacific

At a fundamental level, marketing communication is going through one of the most significant changes influenced by the "Internet of things." For too long, the industry has been using standard demographics as a means to segment, target, and communicate to audiences. For starters, correlation of demographics to behavior is slowly fading away. That age, income, and occupation type of variables are no longer homogenous in predicting that consumer's behavior. This is more pronounced in the online ecosystem. An individual's influences, likes, context, and behavior best reflect his or her disposition toward a brand, its communication, and the resultant need for a call to act. The second-most-important shift (largely as a fallout of the first, mentioned above) is the declining predictability in the path to purchase or the journey a consumer makes from the time he searches for a particular product to the time he actually makes a purchase.

To a larger extent, if one really projects the above two influences—diversified targeting and dynamic path to purchase—we are now entering a new era in marketing communications, where when the individual's identity is reasonably known (better than some of the basic demographics), the nature of communication, the time at which it is delivered, and the format of the same can be customized to provide effective targeting where one can follow the user's path to purchase by first becoming his trusted aide, then providing relevant recommendations, helping him to make a good choice, following through after the sale is done, and making the user a loyalist to the brand. Recommendation engines developed by some of the popular online marketers are in these directions, but it will all finally come down to the veracity of the algorithm that is being deployed and the success of the same.

And now all this means that the sheer volume of data that one needs to assemble, integrate, and analyze has exploded beyond any comparison. In my personal view, the marketing ecosystem is simply not ready to manage this "data deluge." Last time there was a deluge, Noah built an ark, not a bridge. Marketers need to build their own ark for their own enterprise. And to build an ark that can stand the test of time, one needs to deploy superior technology—and here we go: Marketing and IT need to collide and collaborate more than ever before. There are too many companies that are trying to solve this collision/collaboration today, but at the moment, the parts are more distracting than the sum, and hence the gestalt is still sorely missing.

A successful marketing organization should therefore first invest in a "future-proof" architecture that manages data—across the trinity of enterprise, media, and publicly available but anonymized data. Second, such an organization needs to stay ahead of the game with technology that integrates and manages social, mobile, and analytics all from the cloud (where things will eventually sit). And finally, such an organization needs to have talent who can straddle and perform across all the marketing functions with ease but also have their own "passion vertical" to focus and excel.

These are exciting times. Stay young. Stay relevant. Stay focused.

A

Sample Worksheets for Dynamic Ad Campaigns

Setting up personalized ad campaigns can seem overly complex and daunting, given the number of variables and decisions involved, ranging from what data signals to use, what messaging to associate with each individual profile, how to measure, how to optimize, etc.

As with any other complex undertaking, developing a process for how to approach these campaigns can go a long way toward ensuring the success of the campaign and the sanity of all those involved in it.

In this book I describe some of the process and technology elements involved in setting up a personalized advertising campaign. This appendix contains worksheets that are representative of the kinds of tools a team should develop to streamline the process. (Some examples are filled in to demonstrate what you can do.) Since there are several stakeholders in these campaigns, these worksheets serve both to organize and communicate across the client and creative, media planning, dynamic ad platform, and media partners.

Once the campaign launches, these worksheets will also enable easy optimization and analysis of results since all of the key information regarding the campaign is easily accessible.

Personalized advertising is evolving rapidly, and so we expect that these kinds of worksheets and tools will evolve rapidly.

For the latest with these kinds of tools and worksheets, visit www. jivox.com/dynamicads.

Personalized Ads Strategy Worksheet

A personalized ads strategy worksheet can be used to provide a 30,000-foot view of the kinds of data signals and types of rules that could be used to drive engagement. It is often the result of a brainstorm and some ideation cycles between the brand, the creative team, the media team, and the dynamic advertising platform provider (e.g., Jivox).

This worksheet allows everyone a glimpse into the overall strategy and scope of the personalized ad campaign and what kinds of data, assets, and copy development work will be needed in the course of the campaign.

This worksheet will also form the key input into the rest of the process and keep all parties informed on the strategy for the campaign.

JW Personalized Ads Strategy Worksheet

Trigger	Trigger Values	Core Rules Needed	Optional Rules	Number of Creative Groups
Holidays	1. Labor Day 2. Columbus Day 3. Halloween	Day-wise	a.m./p.m.	6 (assuming a.m./p.m. is used)
Twitter trends	Dynamically injected, updated in 24 hours. Text length limited by size of creative. No rules, national coverage.			Dynamic.
Weather	Local weather conditions	Rules for "Hot," "Warm," "Windy," "Muggy," "Cool," "Sunny"		6
Entertainment	Entertainment events	Rules for DMA × dates		As many as DMA × date combos chosen plus one generic

Trigger	Trigger Values	Core Rules Needed	Optional Rules	Number of Creative Groups
Sports	Sporting events	Rules for DMA × dates	Win/loss by home team.	As many as DMA × date combos chosen plus one generic. Optionally double creative based on home team win/loss.

Trigger Worksheets

Trigger worksheets need to be developed for each of the data signals and the different values they can have (or that you want to utilize in the campaign). Keep in mind that a single data signal like weather could have literally hundreds of possible trigger conditions—the various values for temperature, precipitation, humidity, wind speed, pollen count, etc.

One of the first steps, of course, is to identify which of these trigger values make sense to the brand and then flesh out the detailed trigger rules that would be used from that trigger value.

For a beverage brand (e.g., Starbucks), temperature may be a good trigger value as people switch between warm and cold drinks based on temperature. An allergy brand, on the other hand, would probably focus on pollen counts.

Once the trigger values are identified, this worksheet would enable the creative team and copywriter to build messaging to match the trigger values. This is a very detail-oriented process but can avoid the need for creative approvals on every single variant of the advertisement as this approved copy can be used to dynamically populate the ads without having to go through creative approval once again.

Next we provide some examples of how this was done for various weather conditions, sporting events, and entertainment events. In these examples, you can almost see the campaigns come to life as you imagine yourself in New York City on a cold day, seeing a brand's advertisement literally speak to you. This is the power of personalized advertising. What we are doing here is developing a script for the dialogue we would like to have when we (the brand) virtually meet a current or potential consumer of our brand.

We have all been in situations where we were about to meet someone important—a future boss or a date we hoped to impress. We have spent hours thinking of all the clever things we could say, all the interesting observations we could make, all the knowledge we could exhibit, and, most importantly, how we could appear smart and funny.

Speaking of smart and funny, whenever a person is asked what he or she would like in an ideal life partner, smart and funny almost always seem to feature in the list of desires. Of course, good looking, mature, caring, etc., also appear to be important, and so this process is very similar in that the brand needs to put some thought into how it wants to be perceived when a consumer sees its advertisement.

The following worksheet is for weather, so in this case, selecting the right weather triggers is critical. It is always best to not pick absolute values (e.g., you don't want to make an exact temperature a trigger as it may not occur very frequently) but instead to use ranges wherever possible. Also keep in mind what you want to say for the opposite condition; the answer may simply be to say nothing, in which case a default/generic creative message will need to be served.

Weather Data Signal Trigger Worksheet

Current Weather Conditions	Tag Line Messaging	Image/Animation
Very hot (over 90 degrees)	Hot? Nice time to toast to tailgating and try a JW on ice!	Sizzling animation
Very cold (under 30 degrees)	Freezing? Toast to tailgating and warm up with JW.	Frozen face animation
Raining (priority over temperature)	Raining? Toast to tailgating and warm up with a JW.	Rain animation

Current Weather Conditions	Tag Line Messaging	Image/Animation
Snowing (priority over temperature)	Take the sting out of the snow. Toast to tailgating and warm up with JW.	Snow animation
Perfect weather (sunny, moderate temp)	Nice out? Toast to tailgating with JW and feel nice inside, too.	Sunny/blue sky animation
Default weather creative	The perfect companion to a tailgate, JW	Happy face

For holidays, there are some great messaging opportunities. The following worksheet shows some examples. For holidays (e.g., Thanksgiving, Christmas, etc.), it may be useful to also have some visuals depicting each holiday.

Holiday Data Signal Trigger Worksheet

Holiday	Start Date	End Date	Tag Line Messaging
Labor Day pre	8/27/2014	8/31/2014	Here's to the folks who labor to make JW and to those who drink it!
Labor Day of	9/1/2014	9/1/2014	Here's to the folks who labor to make JW and to those who drink it!
Labor Day post	9/2/2014	9/4/2014	Summer's over, but time off is just around the corner. Take advantage and tailgate with JW.
Cheese Pizza Day	9/5/2014	9/5/2014	Looking to share that cheese pizza? Start a tailgate with JW and let the crowd come to you.
Chocolate Milk Shake Day	9/12/2014	9/12/2014	What's sweeter than a chocolate milk shake? Tailgating with JW.
National Cream-Filled Donut Day	9/14/2014	9/14/2014	What's sweeter than a cream-filled donut? Tailgating with JW.

Holiday	Start Date	End Date	Tag Line Messaging
International Talk Like a Pirate Day	9/19/2014	9/19/2014	Ahoy! Start a tailgate with JW, or ye'll be forced to walk the plank!
Miniature Golf Day	9/21/2014	9/21/2014	Finally sunk that elusive hole in one in mini-golf? Start a tailgate with JW and tell everyone all about it.
Elephant Appreciation Day	9/22/2014	9/22/2014	An elephant never forgets how fun tailgating is, and neither will you if you try JW.
National Cherries Jubilee Day	9/24/2014	9/24/2014	What's sweeter than cherries jubilee? Tailgating with JW.
National Comic Book Day	9/25/2014	9/25/2014	Want to be a real superhero? Go start a tailgate with JW.
World Smile Day	10/3/2014	10/3/2014	Put a smile on your face and celebrate the first Friday of the month tailgating with JW.
National Frappe Day	10/4/2014	10/4/2014	What's sweeter than your favorite frappe? Tailgating with JW.
Do Something Nice Day	10/5/2014	10/5/2014	Do something nice for yourself and start a tailgate with JW.
Columbus Day pre	10/10/2014	10/12/2014	It may not have been brought over by ship, but Columbus would have been happy to discover tailgating with JW.
National Angel Food Cake Day	10/10/2014	10/10/2014	What's sweeter than angel food cake ? Tailgating with JW.
Columbus Day of	10/13/2014	10/13/2014	It may not have been brought over by ship, but Columbus would have been happy to discover tailgating with JW.
Columbus Day post	10/14/2014	10/15/2014	If Columbus had discovered tailgating with JW in America, he would have stayed.
National Dessert Day	10/14/2014	10/14/2014	What's sweeter than your favorite dessert? Tailgating with JW.

Holiday	Start Date	End Date	Tag Line Messaging
Halloween pre	10/17/2014	10/30/2014	What's scarier than ghosts and witches? Discovering that you've been tailgating without JW.
National Candy Corn Day	10/30/2014	10/30/2014	What's sweeter than candy corn? Tailgating with JW.
Halloween day of	10/31/2014	10/31/2014	What's scarier than ghosts and witches? Discovering that you've been tailgating without JW.
Halloween post	11/1/2014	11/5/2014	What's scarier than ghosts and witches? Discovering that you've been tailgating without JW.
Thanksgiving pre	11/20/2014	11/26/2014	Not sure what you are thankful for this year? Try tailgating with JW, and you'll thank us later.
Thanksgiving	11/27/2014	11/27/2014	Remember to give thanks for tailgating and share JW with family and friends.
Thanksgiving post	11/28/2014	12/3/2014	Thanksgiving's over, but there is always a reason to be thankful for tailgating with JW.

Sporting events are great to work with as the messaging can be very specific and relevant. There are national sporting events that everyone can relate to. There are also local events that give a brand a chance to personalize messages. This kind of personalization makes the brand look really smart and leaves the user wondering "How did they know there was a local lacrosse tournament today?" The following worksheet provides some examples of personalization for sporting events.

Sporting Event Data Trigger Worksheet

Major Sporting Event	Timing	DMA/National	Team	Tag Line Messaging
Campaign end date expected mid-November				
MLB	Leading up to the event	Baltimore	Orioles	Baltimore, get fired up for the first pitch and tailgate with JW.
Per team	After the event			Win or lose, the postgame is always a home run if you celebrate with JW.
	Leading up to the event	Boston	Red Sox	
NFL	Leading up to the event	Buffalo	Bills	Buffalo, take over tailgating and get ready for kickoff with JW.
Per team	After the event			Win or lose, don't fumble the opportunity to keep the tailgating spirit alive with JW.
	Leading up to the event	Miami	Dolphins	Miami, see what all the buzz is about and tailgate with JW.
	After the event			Win or lose, don't get caught scrambling to find the action. Start your own celebration with JW.
				Don't forget to bring JW as you rush to the after-party to celebrate the win.
				Stiff-arm the disappointment of the defeat. Keep the experience alive with JW.

Major Sporting Event	Timing	DMA/National	Team	Tag Line Messaging
	Leading up to the event	New England	Patriots	Boston, see what all the buzz is about and tailgate with JW.
	After the event			Win or lose, don't get caught scrambling to find the action. Start your own celebration with JW
	Leading up to the event	New York	Jets	New York, see what all the buzz is about and tailgate with JW.
	After the event			Win or lose, don't get caught scrambling to find the action. Start your own celebration with JW
	Leading up to the event	Baltimore	Ravens	Baltimore, see what all the buzz is about and tailgate with JW.
College football	Leading up to the event	Cincinnati	American Athletic	Gear up for the gridiron and fly straight to the tailgate with JW.
Per team	During the event			Win or lose, touch down at the postgame tailgate with JW.
	After the event			Win or lose, don't get caught scrambling to find the action. Start your own celebration with JW.
US Open	Leading up to the event	National		Score an advantage with JW on ice.
	During the event			Thinking of JW while the balls fly.
	After the event			Don't miss the after-party; follow the crowds to JW.

Major Sporting Event	Timing	DMA/National	Team	Tag Line Messaging
Ryder Cup	Leading up to the event	National		You could miss the birdie; head on to the game warmed up with JW.
	During the event			Thinking of JW while the balls fly.
	After the event			Don't miss the after-party; follow the crowds to JW.
NASCAR Geico 400	Leading up to the event	National		Ready for the race? You will be with JW.
	During the event			Thinking of JW while the tires spin.
	After the event			Race to the after-party; JW is waiting.
Presidents Cup	Leading up to the event	National		You could miss the birdie; head on to the game warmed up with JW.
	During the event			Thinking of JW while the balls fly.
	After the event			Don't miss the after-party; follow the crowds to JW.
NASCAR Hollywood Casino 400	Leading up to the event	National		Ready for the race? You will be with JW.
	During the event			Thinking of JW while the tires spin.
	After the event			Race to the after-party; JW is waiting.

Major Sporting Event	Timing	DMA/National	Team	Tag Line Messaging
NASCAR BofA 400	Leading up to the event	National		Ready for the race? You will be with JW.
	During the event			Thinking of JW while the tires spin.
	After the event			Don't miss the after-party; race the crowds to JW.
Ironman World Championship	Leading up to the event	National		Run, don't walk to your JW.
	During the event			All this running, you need a break with JW.
	After the event			Run, don't walk to your JW; you've earned it.
Chicago Marathon	Leading up to the event	National		Run, don't walk to your JW.
	During the event			All this running, you need a break with JW.
	After the event			Run, don't walk to your JW; you've earned it.
NASCAR Camping World RV Sales 500	Leading up to the event	National		Ready for the race? You will be with JW.
	During the event			Thinking of JW while the tires spin.
	After the event			Don't miss the after-party; race the crowds to JW.

Major Sporting Event	Timing	DMA/National	Team	Tag Line Messaging
World Series	Leading up to the event	National		Warm up for the game with a JW.
	During the event			What goes well with a ballpark frank? JW on ice.
	After the event			Win or lose, don't get caught scrambling to find the action. Start your own celebration with JW.
NASCAR Goody's Headache Relief Shot 500	Leading up to the event	National		Ready for the race? You will be with JW.
	During the event			Thinking of JW while the tires spin.
	After the event			Don't miss the after-party; race the crowds to JW.
ATP World Tour Finals	Leading up to the event	National		Score an advantage with JW on ice.
	During the event			Thinking of JW while the balls fly.
	After the event			Don't miss the after-party; follow the crowds to JW.
NYC Marathon	Leading up to the event	National		Run, don't walk to your JW.
	During the event			All this running, you need a break with JW.
	After the event			Keep running to your JW; you've earned it.

Entertainment events are also great opportunities for personal-ized messaging. Events can again be either national or local. Popping in the name of a local artist or venue could make an advertisement look very personalized.

Entertainment Event Data Trigger Worksheet

Major Entertainment Event	Event Type	Genre of Music	City/ National	City
Bumbershoot	Music concert	Mixed, including hip-hop and alterna-tive rock	City	Seattle, WA
http://bumbershoot. org			City	
			City	
LouFest	Music festival	Mixed, including hip-hop and alterna-tive rock	City	St. Louis, MO
www.loufest.com			City	
			City	
Boston Calling Fall	Music concert	Mixed, including hip-hop and alterna-tive rock	City	Boston, MA
http://fall.bostoncall-ing.com			City	
			City	
Riot Fest Chicago	Music concert	Mixed, including hip-hop and alterna-tive rock	City	Chicago, IL
http://riotfest.org			City	
			City	
Forever Never Land	Music concert	Mixed, including hip-hop, alternative rock, and dance	City	San Luis Obispo, CA
www.forevernever-land.us			City	
Sunset Strip Music Festival	Music festival	Mixed, including electronic, rock, indie rock, and R&B	City	Los Angeles, CA

Major Entertainment Event	Event Type	Genre of Music	City/ National	City
www.sunsetstripmusicfestival.com			City	
			City	
Riot Fest Denver	Music concert	Mixed, including hip-hop, electronic, rock, and indie rock	City	Denver, CO
http://riotfest.org			City	
			City	
Austin City Limits	Music concert	Mixed, including - hip-hop, electronic, rock, and indie rock	City	Austin, TX
http://www.aclfestival.com			City	
			City	
A3C Hip Hop Festival	Music festival	Hip-hop	City	Atlanta, GA
http://www.a3cfestival.com			City	
			City	
Treasure Island	Music concert	Mixed, including hip-hop, electronic, rock, and indie rock	City	San Francisco, CA
http://treasureislandfestival.com			City	
			City	
Voodoo Music Experience	Music concert	Mixed, including hip-hop, electronic, rock, and indie rock	City	New Orleans, LA
http://worshipthemusic.com			City	
			City	
Fun Fun Fun Fest	Music festival	Mixed, including hip-hop, electronic, rock, and indie rock	City	Austin, TX
http://funfunfunfest.com			City	

Unlike all the above data signals and trigger events, the one data signal that cannot be preplanned is social media trends. We simply don't know what is going to be the chatter on social media—and that's why the following worksheet is blank. This worksheet can be filled out each week, based on the top trends on Facebook or Twitter. Both Facebook and Twitter report national and local trends, so it is possible to get very granular and specific to a locale. A process you can follow is to provide the brand team with the top trends and have the team develop messaging and then feed it back into the personalized advertisements dynamically each week so they always reflect the currently trending topics on Twitter.

Twitter Trends Data Trigger Worksheet

Trend	Dates	DMAs/ National	Tag Line Messaging	Images/Animation

Glossary

1×1 pixel   A measurement commonly used in advertising to record metrics across systems without using complex APIs. When a reportable event occurs in one system, it invokes a 1×1 pixel (a URL that returns a single transparent pixel), which in turn invokes a URL that reports that event to the receiving system.

A/B testing   A simple optimization technique that is often used in personalized advertising to compare and optimize two creative variations that are run at the same time to try to determine which one is performing better.

ad (advertising) ID   A mechanism Apple and Google have provided in their mobile operating systems to allow advertisements to track users without using personally identifiable information from the devices.

ad production   The process of developing a creative concept and assets into a digital advertisement that can be delivered to users. This process is usually performed in an ad studio associated with an ad serving platform.

ad tag   A piece of code (usually a combination of HTML and JavaScript) that is placed on the website of a media publisher to retrieve an advertisement from an ad server so it can be displayed on the page when a user visits the page.

API (application programming interface)   An interface that allows software programs to communicate without knowing internal details about each other. Two companies or teams can work completely independently and yet have their software work together as long as they develop and communicate an API that is used to exchange information between the two.

artificial intelligence   A discipline within computer science that seeks to enable computers to learn, speak, and behave like humans. Speech recognition, fingerprint matching, facial recognition, and other applications have become possible using artificial intelligence techniques.

attribution The process of giving credit to a particular marketing activity in causing a "sale" or "conversion." A brand might use email, TV, print, digital ads, social media, etc., to promote a product but wants to know how much credit each channel should get for causing a sale. Some channels (e.g., TV) can only be measured indirectly, while click-based conversions can be directly measured.

beacon A small transmitter that is capable of transmitting some information about itself and its location, typically using a Bluetooth transmitter. A receiving device can then compute the user's precise location and use that for various applications. This technology is typically based on the Apple iBeacon standard to deliver location-aware messages to mobile apps and devices.

Big Data The collection, storage, and processing of very large amounts of data for various applications. Big Data is called out from regular data processing because it requires a different set of technologies for processing the data because traditional database, query, and reporting software often cannot scale well enough to process such large volumes of data, especially when the results may be required in near real time.

Bluetooth A wireless transmission standard developed and used for transmitting information over very short distances, using a very low-power transmitter. Bluetooth has been used extensively with mobile devices to allow them to communicate with other devices in their proximity.

CDN (content delivery network) A network, usually provided by a cloud infrastructure like Amazon, Google, Akamai, IBM, etc., that is used to ensure that files and assets are delivered quickly, regardless of the distance of the user from where the file is stored.

click-through A user's clicking an ad in such a manner that it takes the user to the brand's website. This is an important but not exclusive measure of ad performance.

CMS (content management system) A specialized database system that stores content and makes it easy to retrieve on demand. Personalized advertising platforms usually employ a CMS to make it easy to efficiently swap out content in an ad.

conversion tracking Tracking of when and how a "sale" occurred. This is typically used in online sales where if a used clicked on an ad and then purchased the product, that is considered a conversion.

cookie A very small file that code on a web page or a digital advertisement can create that will be saved by the user's web browser. This file will remain for some time and can contain some information about the user. A cookie cannot access anything on the user's system; it is not an active piece of code and so by itself cannot really do anything. It can, however, be used by advertisers to re-target or re-message users based on their browsing habits.

cookie sync   A process by which two sources of data share that data without sharing any personally identifiable information about the user. Most data management platforms use this method to provide or exchange data.

cookieless environment   An environment where it is not possible to use cookies as identifiers of the user. Mobile devices are an example. Newer technology that uses other device information is generally replacing cookies in the mobile environment.

CRM (customer relationship management) system   A software package that allows a brand to store and track information about interactions with its customers. CRM systems often provide valuable insights into customer preferences that can be used for marketing.

data trigger   A condition that can be detected and used for personalizing an advertisement or user experience.

DCO (dynamic creative optimization)   The earliest form of personalized digital advertising, in which brands created a set of messages and creative concepts and then used data to understand which ones performed well so they could use more of that.

default   A creative variant that is served when no rule is true, in order to ensure that some ad creative is rendered. Rules should generally be designed to minimize the number of times a default is served, but a default should always be available to serve if no other creative is appropriate or available.

DI (direct index)   An index used to look up dynamic assets in a file or database for serving up dynamic messaging or creative assets

DMP (data management platform)   A piece of software that is able to efficiently catalog, store, and make available vast amounts of data that have been processed and categorized for use in targeted or personalized marketing.

DSP (demand-side platform)   A technology platform used by media buyers that automates the buying of media by providing an auction model where buyers can specify a price and other characteristics of media they would like to purchase, and the platform will automatically bid for such inventory and execute the campaign to parameters set in the platform.

Flash   A programming language that came into use in the early days of the web as a way of performing animations and rich experiences on the web. The technology is provided by Adobe Systems. It has fallen somewhat out of favor for digital advertising because the Flash language cannot run on mobile devices.

Hadoop   A database technology that is used to store very large amounts of data in a distributed and therefore scalable manner from which analysis can be made for personalization and other activities that require storage and processing of very large amounts of data.

Hive   A database technology that is often used with very large databases to manage querying of data out of those very large databases. Hive has the benefit of utilizing SQL, which makes it easy to write complex data queries to be executed on a database.

HTML (Hypertext Markup Language)   A tag-based declarative language (i.e., not quite a programming language). HTML was the first language used to develop websites by using a simple way to describe the contents of the web page, and it is the foundation on which most websites are built. HTML5 is a new version supported by modern web browsers that adds more sophisticated processing of multimedia like video and animations designed especially for mobile devices.

Internet of Things   A general term used to describe the fact that the Internet is being extended into various devices, making them electronically accessible via the Internet and allowing all of those devices to be connected to and accessible via the Internet.

JavaScript   A scripting language used extensively in programming websites. It is typically used in conjunction with HTML and HTML5 to build websites and increasingly to build ads that will run across devices.

JSON (JavaScript Object Notation)   A descriptive language and communication protocol that allows for different pieces of software to communicate over the Internet in a structured way.

look-alike modeling   A modeling technique that enables the extension of an audience by using fewer qualification criteria or identifying a user by association rather than directly.

machine learning   A term used to describe how computer algorithms and computing power can be used to process data and arrive at conclusions where the human brain cannot. Machine learning uses raw data inputs to "learn" and draw inferences.

media activation   The process of launching or starting an advertising campaign. Media activation traditionally was done manually and now increasingly is being done programmatically.

media planning   The process of determining for a brand what kinds of media should be used to execute an advertising campaign as well as where to purchase the media and how much to pay for it.

metadata   Data about data. Metadata is essentially a structured way of describing something so computers can understand it, and it can also be used to share data between disparate systems and software.

multivariate testing   Testing that is similar to A/B testing but uses many more variables and is therefore much more complex to manage.

OpenRTB   An API that was developed to allow media to be sold and bought programmatically. The API allows for media (advertising impressions) to be bid on and fulfilled electronically.

personalization data store   A database that a brand can build to store all of the internal and external data that would be critical to effectively personalizing advertising to a user.

PII (personally identifiable information)   Information such as name and Social Security number that identifies a particular individual. Data used for dynamic and personalized advertising needs to be sanitized to remove any PII.

predictive modeling   A technique used to predict when a consumer may take some action (e.g., a purchase) by looking at the behavior leading up to that action. Large data sets sometimes have to be analyzed to make predictive modeling work.

rich media   A type of display banner advertisement that delivers a much richer experience than traditional banner ads, by using animations, video, and other multimedia elements to gain engagement from users.

RSS (Really Simple Syndication)   A web standard that allows information to be published in a standard manner so it can be read and consumed by various applications. It is usually provided as a feed of images, text, and clickable descriptions.

rules engine   A piece of technology that allows rules to be defined for when a certain message or creative variation should be delivered to a user. A rules engine also executes a rule at runtime in a scalable and quick manner.

SQL (Structured Query Language)   A language developed in the 1990s that makes it easy to query databases without knowing programming. It uses the concept of rows and columns to retrieve data from a database.

SSP (supply-side platform)   Software that enables publishers to pool all their advertising inventory and make it available for purchase by other platforms. The SSP typically manages pricing and ensures optimal sales of the inventory.

targeting   The practice in digital advertising of using data about users (usually from cookies) to identify the right user to serve an advertisement. This is in contrast to personalization, which seeks to serve an appropriate message to any user an advertisement is served to.

view-through   The process in which a user sees a digital ad for a brand but doesn't click through to purchase but rather just goes to the brand's website either directly or via a search.

wearable technology   Devices that we wear on our person in order to measure things like our sleep patterns, exercise patterns, etc. Wearable technologies collect very personal data that could potentially be used to personalize applications and advertising.

XML (Extensible Markup Language)   A notation that is used to represent data in web applications and on websites.

Index

A

A/B testing, 88
ad development studio, 131
ad IDs, 116
advertising
  assets, 127
  banner formats, 67-68
  billboards, 1-2
  campaigns, launching, 45
  data
    correlating, 18
    limitations of, 17-18
    privacy issues, 18
  data-driven dynamic ads,
    developing, 125-126
  DCO, 39-41
  display banner ads, 2
  event-based dynamic ads, 52
  formats, 8-9, 67
  micro-messaging, 5
  mobile advertising, 69
  native advertising, 35-37
  optimization of personalized
    ads, 87-91
    A/B testing, 88
    machine learning, 89-91
    multivariate testing, 88-89
  paid media advertising, 120

personalization, 2, 35-37
  costs, managing, 85-87
  measuring, 81-84
  programmatic media buying,
    63-66
  ROI, 83-84
personalized ad campaigns,
  planning for, 71
  creative approvals,
    obtaining, 79
  creative canvas, 74-75
  creative production, 75-76
  data signals, identifying,
    71-72
  dynamic data signals,
    defining, 78-79
  key metrics, identifying, 76-77
  optimization criteria,
    identifying, 77-78
  QA process, 79-80
  trigger conditions, identifying,
    72-74
  variables, identifying, 72
reach, 7-10
relevance, increasing, 23-26
site content-powered ads, 94-95
site data, integrating into ad
  content, 95-97